A BRIEF HISTORY FROM THE FOUNDING OF THE CITY

A BRIEF HISTORY FROM THE FOUNDING OF THE CITY

A new translation of Eutropius'
Breviarium Ab Urbe Condita

Brian A. Gibbons

Book design by Brian A. Gibbons

Edited by Jason Huerta

Published by Lulu

The author's website is:

http://www.aburbecondita.com

ISBN 978-1-4357-0541-8

Parentibus meis

Contents

Introduction

Eutropius lived in the fourth century. He accompanied the emperor Julian on a campaign against the Parthians and served under the emperor Valens. He wrote his history around the year 370 and dedicated it to Valens. His book briefly touches on almost every significant Roman personality and event, from the city's founding to Valens' reign, late in the empire. It ends about a century before the fall of Rome. It's more than eleven hundred years of Roman history in under one hundred pages.

Preface

For Master Valens Gothicus Maximus Perpetuus Augustus

In accordance with the wish of your Clemency, I have compiled, in a short narrative and in chronological order, those events in Roman history which are conspicuous in war and peace, from the founding of the city until our own time, and have briefly added those occurrences which stand out as extraordinary in the lives of the leading men, in order that the divine mind of your Serenity may rejoice that it has followed the actions of illustrious men in managing the empire, before it learned of them from reading.

Book I

1. Human memory can hardly recall another empire in the entire world smaller in its beginning or greater in its growth than the Roman Empire, which was begun by Romulus. Romulus was the son of Rhea Silvia, a Vestal Virgin, and, as it was believed, Mars. He was born a twin with his brother Remus. When he was eighteen years old and marauding with a group of shepherds, he established a small city on the Palatine hill, on April 21st, in the third year of the sixth Olympiad, in the three hundred and ninety-fourth year after the destruction of Troy.

2. After founding the city, which he named "Rome" after himself, he did as follows. He took in a large number of the neighboring people and selected one hundred of the older men, with whose counsel he would conduct all matters, and called them "senators" on account of their age. Then, since he and his people did not have wives, he invited all the neighboring tribes of the city of Rome to a show of games and seized their young girls. Wars broke out because of this, and he conquered the Caeninenses, Antemnates, Crustumini, Sabines, Fidenates, and Veians. All of their towns surrounded the city. When he failed to appear after a storm suddenly arose, he was believed to have crossed over to the gods and was deified, in the thirty-seventh year of his reign. Afterwards, in Rome, senators ruled for five days at a time, and a year passed in this way.

3. Afterwards, Numa Pompilius was chosen king. He indeed waged no wars, but benefited the state no less than Romulus, for he established both laws and customs for the Romans, who, for their habit of fighting, were already thought of as robbers and semibarbarians. He also defined the year, which had earlier been without order, into ten months and established countless sacred rites and temples in Rome. He died of illness in the forty-third year of his reign.

4. Tullius Hostilius succeeded him and renewed the wars. He defeated the Albans, who are at the twelfth milestone from the city of Rome. He also overcame in war the Fidenates and Veians, the former of whom are by the sixth milestone from the city, the latter by the eighteenth. He enlarged the city, having added the Caelian hill to it. When he had reigned for thirty-two years, he was struck by a lightning bolt and burned along with his house.

5. After him, Ancus Marcius, the grandson of Numa through his daughter, took control. He fought against the Latins. He added the Aventine hill and the Janiculum to the city. He founded a city by the sea at the mouth of the Tiber, near the sixteenth milestone from the city of Rome. He perished from illness in the twenty-fourth year of his reign.

6. Next, Tarquinius Priscus took over the kingdom. He doubled the number of senators and built the Circus in Rome. He instituted the Roman games which continue to our own time. He conquered the Sabines also, took a large amount of land from them, and joined it to the territory of the city of Rome. He was the first to enter the city in triumph. He built walls and sewers and began the Capitol. In the thirty-eighth year of his reign, he was slain by the sons of Ancus, the king whom he himself had succeeded.

7. Servius Tullius took over after him. He was born from a noblewoman, but one that was a captive and servant. He also subjugated the Sabines. He added three hills to the city: the Quirinal, Viminal, and Esquiline hills; and he dug a ditch around the walls. He was the first to arrange a census of everyone, which up until this time was unheard of throughout the world. Under him, with everyone reported in the census, Rome had eighty-three thousand citizens, including those in the country. He was murdered through the treachery of his son-in-law, Tarquinius Superbus (the son of the king whom he had succeeded), and his own daughter, whom Tarquinius had as a wife.

8. Lucius Tarquinius Superbus, seventh and last of the kings, conquered the Volsci, a tribe which is not far away from the city for those heading to Campania. He subjugated the cities of Gabii and Suessia Pometia, made peace with the Tuscans, and built a temple of Jupiter on the Capitoline hill. Afterwards, while attacking Ardea, a city located by the eighteenth milestone from the city of Rome, he lost his dominion; for his younger son, also named Tarquinius, had violated Lucretia, a most noble and chaste woman who was the wife of Collatinus. After she had complained of this injury to her husband, father, and friends, she killed herself in sight of everyone. Brutus himself, also a relative of Tarquinius, roused the people and removed him from power. Soon, the army, which was besieging the city of Ardea with the king himself, abandoned him as well. When he came to the city, he found the gates closed and himself shut out, and although he had reigned for twenty-four years, he fled with his wife and children. Thus, Rome was ruled by seven kings for two hundred and forty-three years, yet the land the Romans possessed, where it extended furthest, barely reached the fifteenth milestone.

9. Henceforth, they began to have consuls — two in the place of one king, chosen for the reason that if one of them were to be wicked, the other, having similar power, could restrain him. It was also decided that their power should not last longer than a year so that they would not become more insolent by a longer period of power. Those who knew they would be private citizens again after a year would be civil at all times. Therefore, in the first year after the kings were expelled, the consuls were Lucius Junius Brutus, who played the lead role in expelling Tarquinius, and Tarquinius Collatinus, the husband of Lucretia. But Tarquinius Collatinus' position was immediately taken away, for it was resolved that nobody should remain in the city named Tarquinius. Therefore, after receiving his property, he moved away from the city, and in his place, Lucius Valerius Publicola was made consul. However, the expelled King Tarquinius incited a war against the city of Rome, and after collecting many tribes, he fought to be restored to his kingdom.

10. In the first battle, the consul Brutus and Arruns, son of Tarquinius, killed each other, but the Romans left victorious. The Roman matrons mourned a year for Brutus, the defender of their virtue, as if he was a common father to all. Valerius Publicola made Spurius Lucretius Tricipitinus, the father of Lucretia, his colleague, but he died shortly after from illness. He took another colleague for himself, Horatius Pulvillus. Thus, the first year had five consuls since Tarquinius Collatinus left the city because of his name, Brutus died in battle, and Spurius Lucretius died from illness.

11. Again the next year, Tarquinius waged war against the Romans in order to win back his kingdom. He was aided by Porsenna, the king of Tuscia, and almost took Rome but was defeated that time as well. In the third year after the kings were expelled, Tarquinius, since he could not recover his kingdom and Porsenna (who had made peace with the Romans) would not furnish him aid, went to Tusculum, a city not far from Rome, and stayed there for fourteen years as a private citizen, growing old with his wife. In the fourth year after the kings were expelled, the Sabines brought war to the Romans. They were conquered, and a triumph was celebrated. In the fifth year, Lucius Valerius, the colleague of Brutus and a four-time consul, died a natural death. He was so poor that the expense of his burial was paid by coins collected from the populace. The Roman matrons mourned him for a year, just as they had Brutus.

12. In the ninth year after the kings were driven out, when the son-in-law of Tarquinius had assembled a vast army to avenge the injury against his father-in-law, a new office was created in Rome, greater than a consulship, called a "dictatorship." Also in the same year, a "master of horse" was made, who would take orders from the dictator. Nothing is closer to the power of government which your Serenity now holds than the ancient dictatorship, especially when Octavian Augustus, whom we will speak of later, and before him, Caius Caesar, ruled with the title and office of dictator. The first dictator of Rome was Titus Larcius; the first master of horse, Spurius Cassius.

13. In the sixteenth year after the kings were expelled, the people of Rome rose up on the grounds that they were being hard-pressed by the Senate and consuls. They then chose for themselves tribunes of the people, who would act as their own judges and defenders, and by whose protection they would be safe from the Senate and consuls.

14. In the following year, the Volsci renewed the war against the Romans and were defeated in battle. They also lost Corioli, the best city they had.

15. In the eighteenth year after the kings were ejected, Quintus Marcius, the Roman general who had taken Corioli, the city of the Volsci, was expelled from Rome. Angry over this, he hurried to the Volsci themselves and received assistance against the Romans. He defeated the Romans often and advanced all the way to the fifth milestone from the city. He was even about to attack his native city, having already scorned the deputies who had come seeking peace, when his mother Veturia and wife Volumnia came to him from the city. Overcome by their weeping and pleading, he withdrew his army. He was the second leader, after Tarquinius, who had opposed his country.

16. In the consulship of Caius Fabius and Lucius Virginius, three hundred noblemen from the Fabia family undertook a war alone against the Veians, promising the Senate and people that they themselves would finish the whole contest. All of the noblemen, each of whom ought to have been the leader of a great army, set out and fell in battle. Only one male, who could not be brought to the battle on account of his youth, survived from so great a family. After this, a census was held in the city, and it was found that there were one hundred and seventeen thousand, three hundred and nineteen citizens.

17. In the following year, when the Roman army was besieged on Mt. Algidus near the twelfth milestone from the city, Lucius Quintius Cincinnatus was made dictator. He possessed a field of four acres which he cultivated with his own hands. When he was found, busy working and plowing, he wiped off his sweat and put on the toga praetexta [a toga worn by higher magistrates and free-born boys with a purple stripe on its border]. Then, after slaughtering the enemy, he freed the army.

18. In the three hundred and second year after the founding of the city, the consular government ceased, and in the place of two consuls, ten were chosen, called "decemvirs," who would hold the highest power. But although they conducted themselves well in the first year, in the second, one of them, Appius Claudius, attempted to seduce the young daughter of a certain Virginius who was serving honorably at that time on Mt. Algidus against the Latins. She was killed by her father in order to spare her from having to endure the debauchery of the decemvir. After returning to the soldiers, he incited an uprising. The decemvirs were stripped of their power and condemned.

19. In the three hundred and fifteenth year after the founding of the city, the Fidenates rebelled against the Romans. The Veians and their king, Tolumnius, supplied them aid. Both of these cities were quite close to Rome; Fidenae was by the sixth milestone from the city and Veii was by the eighteenth. The Volsci also joined up with them but were conquered by the dictator, Mamercus Aemilius, and the master of horse, Lucius Quintius Cincinnatus. They lost their king as well. Fidenae was taken and destroyed.

20. Twenty years later, the Veians rebelled. Furius Camillius was sent against them as dictator. He first conquered them in battle, then also took their city, the most ancient and richest in Italy, after besieging it for some time. After he took this city, he also took Falisci, a city that was no less noble. But he became unpopular because it was thought that he had divided the plunder unfairly, and for this, he was found guilty and expelled from the state. The Gallic Senones came to the city at once, pursuing the Romans after beating them at the river Allia by the eleventh milestone, and occupied it. Nothing could be defended against them except the Capitol. When the Capitol had been besieged for a long time, and the Romans were suffering from hunger, the Gauls departed, having received gold to desist from the siege. Camillus, who was spending his exile in a nearby city, came upon the Gauls unexpectedly and thoroughly defeated them.

Afterwards, Camillus pursued them and defeated them in such a way that he recovered the gold which they had been given and all the military standards which they had captured. Thus, he entered the city for the third time in triumph and was called the second Romulus, as if he too had been a founder of the city.

Book II

1. In the three hundred and sixty-fifth year since the founding of the city, but the first after it had been captured, the offices were changed. Instead of two consuls, military tribunes with consular power were made. From this time on, the Roman state began to grow; for in the same year, Camillus conquered the state of the Volsci, who had warred against them for seventy years. He also defeated the cities of the Aequi and Sutrini, capturing them after their armies were destroyed, and celebrated three triumphs at the same time.

2. Additionally, Titus Quintius Cincinnatus pursued the Praenestini, a people who had brought war up to the gates of Rome, to the river Allia and defeated them. He joined eight cities that were under them to the Romans; he attacked Praeneste itself and accepted its surrender. All these things were accomplished by him in twenty days, and a triumph was decreed for him.

3. But indeed, the office of military tribune did not last long, for after some time it was resolved that no more would be made, and four years passed in the city in such a way that there were no higher positions of power there. However, military tribunes with consular authority assumed the position again and remained for three years; then consuls were made again.

4. Camillus died in the consulship of Lucius Genucius and Quintus Servilius. Honor second to that of Romulus was given to him.

5. Titus Quintius was sent as dictator against the Gauls, who had come to Italy. They had encamped by the fourth milestone from the city across the river Aniene. There, a most noble young senator, Lucius Manlius, entered into single combat with, and killed, a Gaul who had challenged him. Then, after removing the Gaul's torque [a metal ring worn around the neck], he placed it on his own neck and received for all-time, for himself and his descendants, the surname "Torquatus." The Gauls were routed, and soon after, were defeated by the dictator Caius Sulpicius. Soon after, the Tuscans were defeated by Caius Marcius, and eight thousand captives were led in triumph.

6. A census was held again. Since the Latins, who had been subjugated by the Romans, were unwilling to furnish soldiers, recruits were only taken from the Romans. Ten legions were formed, which came out to sixty thousand or more men in arms. So great was Roman power in warfare, even though the Roman state was still small. After they set out against the Gauls with Lucius Furius as general, a certain Gaul challenged the Romans to send out their best man. A tribune of the soldiers, Marcus Valerius, volunteered, and as he advanced armed, a raven landed on his right shoulder. Soon after, when they were joined in combat, the same raven attacked the eyes of the Gaul with its wings and talons so that he could not see properly. Thus, the Gaul was slain by the tribune Valerius. The raven not only gave Valerius a victory, but also a name, for afterwards, he was called "Corvinus" [a name meaning raven]. He was made consul at twenty-three years of age on account of this deed.

7. The Latins, who had refused to supply soldiers, began also to demand from the Romans that one of the consuls be chosen from their people and the other one from the Roman people. After this was refused, a war was undertaken against the Latins, and they were defeated in a great battle. A triumph was held on account of their subjugation. Statues were placed for the consuls on the rostra for their part in the victory. Also, in the same year, Alexandria was founded by Alexander the Macedonian.

8. Now the Romans were beginning to become powerful; for a war was waged with the Samnites, who were at the one hundred and thirtieth milestone from the city, between Picenum, Campania, and Apulia. Lucius Papirius Cursor set out for the war with the title of dictator. When he returned to Rome, he ordered Quintus Fabius Maximus, the master of horse whom he had left in charge of the army, not to fight while he was absent. After finding a favorable opportunity, Quintus Fabius Maximus fought most successfully and destroyed the Samnites. He was condemned to die by the dictator because he had fought against his orders, but was freed because of his great popularity with the soldiers and people. Such a great uproar arose against Papirius that he himself was almost killed.

9. Afterwards, in the consulship of Titus Veturius and Spurius Postumius, the Samnites defeated the Romans (a great disgrace for them) and sent them under the yoke. However, the peace the Romans made with them out of necessity was ended by the Senate and people. After this, the Samnites were defeated by the consul Lucius Papirius, and seven thousand of them were sent under the yoke. Papirius celebrated a triumph over them. The censor Appius Claudius constructed the Aqua Claudia and the Via Appia at this time. After renewing the war, the Samnites defeated Quintus Fabius Maximus and slew three thousand of his men. Later, his father, Fabius Maximus, while serving as his lieutenant, defeated the Samnites and took many of their towns. Then, both consuls, Publius Cornelius Rufinus and Manius Curius Dentatus, were sent against the Samnites and wore them out in a series of large battles. They then ended the war which had lasted for forty-nine years. There was no other enemy within Italy who had tested Roman strength more.

10. After several years time, the Gauls again joined with the Tuscans and Samnites against the Romans, but as they were marching towards Rome, they were annihilated by the consul Cnaeus Cornelius Dolabella.

11. War was declared at this time against the Tarentines, who still live at the end of Italy, because they caused injury to some Roman ambassadors. The Tarentines requested assistance from Pyrrhus, king of Epirus, who was descended from the line of Achilles. He soon came to Italy, and for the first time, the Romans fought with an enemy from across the sea. The consul Publius Valerius Laevinius was sent against him. Laevinius captured several scouts of Pyrrhus and ordered for them to be led around the camp and shown the whole army. Then, they were to be released in order to announce to Pyrrhus everything the Romans were doing. Soon, they joined in battle and Pyrrhus was on the verge of flight, but he was victorious due to the use of elephants, which were unknown to the Romans and which they feared. Soon after, darkness brought an end to the fighting, and Laevinius fled in the night. Pyrrhus took eighteen hundred Roman prisoners, treated them honorably, and buried the dead. When he saw the Roman dead lying with wounds in front and fierce expressions even in death, he was said to have raised his hands to the sky and lamented that he could have been the master of the whole world if it had been his fortune to have soldiers such as these.

12. Then, after joining with the Samnites, Lucanians, and Bruttians, Pyrrhus headed towards Rome, devastating everything by fire and sword, and laying waste Campania before arriving at Praeneste, by the eighteenth milestone from the city. Soon after, he retreated to Campania out of fear of an army that was following him with a consul. Delegates were sent to him for the sake of redeeming the captives and were honorably received by him. He sent the captives to Rome without ransom. Pyrrhus so admired Fabricius, one of the Roman delegates, that when he found out he was poor, he tried to entice Fabricius to cross over to his side by promising him one fourth of his kingdom, but he was scorned by Fabricius. This filled Pyrrhus with such admiration of the Romans that he sent an ambassador, a distinguished man named Cineas, to seek peace on fair terms. The terms were that Pyrrhus would keep only that part of Italy which he had already taken by arms.

13. The Romans were unhappy with the peace terms. Cineas returned to Pyrrhus with a reply from the Senate that there would be no peace unless he left Italy. Then, the Romans ordered that all the prisoners that Pyrrhus had sent back to Rome should be regarded as infamous because they had been captured while armed. They would not be able to return to their former standing until they had brought back the spoils of two slain enemy soldiers. When Pyrrhus asked Cineas what type of place he had found Rome to be, he replied that he had seen a nation of kings, and indeed, almost every man there was the type of man that Pyrrhus alone was considered to be in Epirus and the rest of Greece. The consuls Publius Sulpicius and Decius Mus were sent as generals against Pyrrhus. After the battle was joined, Pyrrhus was wounded and his elephants were killed. Twenty thousand of Pyrrhus' men were cut down as opposed to only five thousand of the Romans. Pyrrhus was forced to flee to Tarentum.

14. After a year's time, Fabricius (who earlier, as a delegate, could not be bribed although he had been offered one fourth of Pyrrhus' kingdom) was dispatched against Pyrrhus. Since he and the king had camps close to one another, Pyrrhus' physician came to him at night, promising he would kill Pyrrhus with poison if something was offered to him in return. Fabricius ordered him to be led back to his master in chains and for Pyrrhus to be told of the threats against his life that the physician had made. Subsequently, the king, so impressed by Fabricius, is reported to have said, "Fabricius is a man who would be harder to divert from his integrity than the sun from its course." The king then set out for Sicily. Fabricius held a triumph after defeating the Lucanians and Samnites. Next, the consuls Manius Curius Dentatus and Cornelius Lentulus were sent against Pyrrhus. Curius fought against him, savaged his army, sent him fleeing to Tarentum, and took his camp. On that day, twenty-three thousand of the enemy were slain. Curius triumphed during his consulship and was the first to bring elephants, four in number, to Rome. Pyrrhus soon left Tarentum and was killed at Argos, a city of Greece.

15. In the four hundred and sixty-first year since the founding of the city, during the consulship of Caius Fabius Licinius and Caius Claudius Canina, ambassadors, sent by Ptolemy, came to Rome from Alexandria and obtained from the Romans the friendship which they had sought.

16. In the consulship of Quintus Olgunius and Caius Fabius Pictor, the Picentes started a war and were defeated by the next consuls, Publius Sempronius and Appius Claudius. A triumph was held over them. The Romans also founded the cities of Ariminum in Gaul and Beneventum in Samnium.

17. During the consulship of Marcus Atilius Regulus and Lucius Julius Libo, war was declared against the Sallentines of Apulia. The Brundisians were taken along with their city, and a triumph was celebrated over them.

18. In the four hundred and seventy-seventh year, although the name of the city of Rome was already famous, arms had still not yet been brought outside of Italy. Therefore, in order to determine the strength of the Romans, a census was held. The number of citizens was found to be two hundred and ninety-two thousand, three hundred and thirty-four, although the wars had never ceased since the founding of the city. For the first time, war was undertaken against the Africans, in the consulship of Appius Claudius and Quintus Fulvius. The Romans fought in Sicily, and Appius Claudius held a triumph over the Africans and King Hiero of Sicily.

19. In the following year, during the consulship of Valerius Marcus and Otacilius Crassus, the Romans accomplished great things in Sicily. The Tauromenitani, Catinenses, and fifty additional cities were received into allegiance. In the third year, the war against Hiero, king of the Sicilians, was resolved. He, along with all of the Syracusan nobility, obtained peace from the Romans and paid them two hundred silver talents. The Africans were defeated in Sicily, and for the second time, a triumph was held in Rome over them.

20. In the fifth year of the Punic war, which was waged against the Africans, during the consulship of Caius Duillius and Cnaeus Cornelius Asina, the Romans fought for the first time at sea after building beaked ships which they called "Liburnian" galleys. The consul Cornelius was undone by treachery. Duillius defeated the Carthaginian commander after joining in battle. He captured thirty-one ships and sank fourteen; he took prisoner seven thousand of the enemy and killed three thousand. No other victory was more pleasing to the Romans because they were already invincible on land, but now they were also powerful at sea. In the consulship of Caius Aquilius

Florus and Lucius Scipio, Scipio ravaged Corsica and Sardinia, led away many thousands of prisoners from there, and celebrated a triumph.

21. In the consulship of Lucius Manlius Vulso and Marcus Atilius Regulus, the war was taken to Africa. A battle was fought at sea against the Carthaginian commander Hamilcar, and he was defeated, for he retreated after losing sixty-four ships. The Romans lost twenty-two ships. After the Romans crossed over into Africa, the first city they reached, Clypea, surrendered to them. The consuls proceeded all the way to Carthage, and after causing much destruction, Manlius returned to Rome victorious, bringing back twenty-seven thousand prisoners, and Atilius Regulus remained in Africa. Regulus drew up his army for battle against the Africans. He was victorious fighting against three Carthaginian generals, killing eighteen thousand of the enemy, capturing five thousand men and eighteen elephants, and receiving seventy-four cities into allegiance. The defeated Carthaginians then sought peace from the Romans. Since Regulus was unwilling to grant this except under the harshest conditions, the Africans sought assistance from the Lacedaemonians. The Lacedaemonians sent Xanthippus, and with him as general, the Roman general Regulus was defeated in a great slaughter. Only two thousand men escaped from the whole Roman army. Five hundred men were captured with Regulus, thirty thousand were slain, and Regulus himself was thrown into chains.

22. In the consulship of Marcus Aemilius Paulus and Servius Fulvius Nobilior, both Roman consuls departed for Africa with a fleet of three hundred ships and defeated the Africans in a naval battle. The consul Aemilius sank one hundred and four of the enemy's ships, captured thirty with soldiers, and killed or captured fifteen thousand of the enemy. He enriched his soldiers with an immense amount of booty. Africa would have been conquered then, but food was so scarce that the army could not stay longer. As the consuls were returning around Sicily with the victorious fleet, they were shipwrecked. There was such a great storm that out of four hundred and sixty-four ships, only eighty could be saved. So great a storm at sea was previously unheard of. The Romans repaired two hundred ships right away, and their spirit was not broken by any of this.

23. The consuls Cnaeus Servilius Caepio and Caius Sempronius Blaesus departed for Africa with two hundred and sixty ships and captured several cities. As they were returning with a great amount of booty, they were shipwrecked. Therefore, since the Romans were unhappy with the continuous naval disasters, the Senate decreed that they would abstain from fighting at sea, and only sixty ships would be kept for the protection of Italy.

24. In the consulship of Lucius Caecilius Metellus and Caius Furius Placidus, Metellus defeated the leader of the Africans in Sicily, who had one hundred and thirty elephants and large forces with him. Metellus killed twenty thousand of the enemy, captured twenty-six elephants, and collected the rest of the elephants, which were wandering around, with the help of the Numidians, whom he had for assistance. He brought the elephants to Rome with great pomp, and one hundred and thirty of them filled all the roads. After these disasters, the Carthaginians sought from Regulus, the general whom they had captured, that he depart for Rome, make peace with the Romans, and arrange an exchange of captives.

25. When Regulus arrived at Rome, he was led into the Senate and did not act at all like a Roman. He said that from the day he had been captured by the Africans, he had ceased to be Roman. He prevented his wife from embracing him and urged the Senate not to make peace with the Carthaginians, for they had no hope left after being broken by so many disasters. He himself was not so important that so many thousands of prisoners should be returned in exchange for an old man like him and a few others who had been captured. He obtained his request, and nobody gave the Africans seeking peace an audience. The Romans offered to keep him in Rome, but he returned to Carthage. He said that he would not remain in the city since he could no longer hold the position of an honorable citizen after having served the Africans. Therefore, after returning to Africa, he was killed by every type of torture.

26. In the consulship of Publius Claudius Pulcher and Lucius Junius,

Claudius fought, although the auspices were unfavorable, and was defeated by the Carthaginians. Out of two hundred and twenty ships, he fled with thirty. Ninety ships were captured with soldiers on board, and the rest of them were sunk. The other consul also lost a fleet, this time by shipwreck. However, his army was unhurt because the shore was nearby.

27. During the consulship of Caius Lutatius Catulus and Aulus Postumius Albinus, in the twenty-third year of the Punic war, Catulus managed the war against the Africans. He set out with three hundred ships to Sicily. The Africans prepared four hundred ships against him. Never before had so many men fought at sea. Lutatius Catulus boarded his ship, weak from being wounded in an earlier battle. The Romans fought with great valor near Lilybaeum, a city of Sicily. Sixty-three Carthaginian ships were taken, one hundred and twenty-five were sunk, thirty-two thousand of their men were captured, thirteen thousand were slain, and a staggering amount of gold, silver, and booty was taken by the Romans. This battle was fought on March 10th. The Carthaginians immediately asked for peace, and it was granted to them. The Roman prisoners who were being held by the Carthaginians were returned. The Carthaginians asked permission to buy back their prisoners. The Senate ordered the ones who were in the custody of the state to be given back without cost. Moreover, those who were held by private citizens were to be returned to Carthage and their owners compensated, but they would be paid from the public treasury rather than by the Carthaginians.

28. Quintus Lutatius and Aulus Manlius were elected as consuls and waged war against the Falisci, a once powerful people of Italy. Both consuls together finished the war within six days of arriving. They slaughtered fifteen thousand of the enemy and granted peace to the rest, but took half of their land from them.

Book III

1. After the Punic war (which dragged on for twenty-three years) came to an end, the Romans, now very famous, sent ambassadors to King Ptolemy of Egypt to offer assistance because King Antiochus of Syria had started a war against him. He thanked the Romans but accepted no assistance because the war had already ended. At the same time, Hiero, the most powerful king of Sicily, came to Rome to watch the games and gave a gift to the people of two hundred thousand modii [a measure of about two gallons] of wheat.

2. In the consulship of Lucius Cornelius Lentulus and Fulvius Flaccus, the same consulship in which Hiero had come to Rome, war was waged inside Italy against the Ligurians, and a triumph was held over them. In addition, the Carthaginians tried to renew the war by inciting the Sardinians (who by the terms of the peace treaty were bound to obey the Romans) to rebel. However, a delegation of Carthaginians came to Rome and procured peace.

3. In the consulship of Titus Manlius Torquatus and Caius Atilius Bulcus, a triumph was held over the Sardinians, and having made peace with all their neighbors, the Romans were not engaged in any war. This had only happened to them once (during the reign of Numa Pompilius) since the founding of the city.

4. The consuls Lucius Postumius Albinus and Cnaeus Fulvius Centumalus waged war against the Illyrians, and after capturing many of their cities, they also accepted the surrender of their kings. Then, for the first time, a triumph was celebrated over the Illyrians.

5. When Lucius Aemilius was consul, vast numbers of Gauls crossed the Alps. All Italy united behind the Romans, and as the historian Fabius (who was present in that war) related, eight hundred thousand men were assembled for war. The war, however, was successfully concluded by the consul alone. Forty thousand of the enemy were slain, and a triumph was decreed for Aemilius.

6. Several years later, during the consulship of Marcus Claudius Marcellus and Cnaeus Cornelius Scipio, a war was fought and concluded within Italy against the Gauls. Marcellus fought with a small group of cavalry and killed Viridomarus, the king of the Gauls, with his own hands. Afterwards, with his colleague, he killed a large number of Gauls, stormed Milan, and carried a great amount of plunder back to Rome. Marcellus carried the spoils of the Gauls on a pole on his shoulders in his triumph.

7. In the consulship of Marcus Minucius Rufus and Publius Cornelius, war was waged against the Istrians because they had plundered some Roman ships that were carrying grain. They were completely subdued. In the same year, the second Punic war was started by Hannibal, the Carthaginian general, against the Romans. Hannibal, at twenty years of age, having gathered forty thousand men, moved against Saguntum, a city friendly to the Romans. Roman delegates demanded that Hannibal abstain from war, but he would not meet with them. The Romans also sent delegates to Carthage in order for Hannibal to be ordered not to wage war against the allies of the Roman people. The Carthaginians gave a harsh response. Meanwhile, the Saguntians succumbed to hunger and were taken by Hannibal, who inflicted the most severe punishments on them.

8. At that time, Publius Cornelius Scipio set out for Spain with his army, and Titus Sempronius set out for Sicily. War was declared against the Carthaginians. Hannibal left his brother Hasdrubal in Spain and crossed the Pyrenees. He opened a path for himself through the Alps which, up until that time, were impassable in that area. It is reported that he brought eighty thousand infantry, ten thousand cavalry, and thirty-seven elephants to Italy. Many Ligurians and Gauls also joined him. After finding out about Hannibal's arrival in Italy, Sempronius Gracchus sent his army from Sicily to Ariminum.

9. Publius Cornelius Scipio was the first to encounter Hannibal. After the battle was joined, Scipio's army was routed, and he himself returned to his camp wounded. Sempronius Gracchus and Hannibal fought at the river Trebia, and he also was defeated. Many in Italy surrendered to Hannibal. As Hannibal was going to Tuscia, he met the consul Flaminius and killed him. Twenty-five thousand of the Romans were slaughtered, and the rest were scattered. The Romans then sent Quintus Fabius Maximus against Hannibal. He broke Hannibal's momentum by avoiding battle and soon, upon finding a favorable opportunity, defeated him.

10. In the five hundred and fortieth year since the founding of the city, Lucius Aemilius Paulus and Publius Terentius Varro succeeded Fabius and were sent against Hannibal. Fabius warned both consuls that they would not be able to defeat the skillful and impetuous general, Hannibal, unless they avoided entering a pitched battle. But due to the impatience of the consul Varro, even though the other consul Paulus was in disagreement, they joined in battle near a village named Cannae in Apulia, and both consuls were defeated by Hannibal. In this battle, three thousand of the Africans perished, and a great part of Hannibal's army was wounded. However, in no other battle during the Punic wars did the Romans suffer more. In this battle, the consul Aemilius Paulus and twenty men of consular or praetorian rank perished. Thirty senators, three hundred noblemen, forty thousand soldiers, and thirty-five hundred cavalry were captured or slain. None of the Romans, however, even amid these disasters, considered mentioning peace. Slaves were freed and made soldiers, something which had never happened before.

11. After that battle, many cities which were under the Romans switched their allegiance to Hannibal. Hannibal offered the Romans the chance to redeem their prisoners, but the Senate replied that those citizens who allowed themselves to be taken while they were still armed were unimportant. Hannibal killed all of them afterwards by various tortures and sent three modii of gold rings, which he had pulled off the hands of Roman knights, senators, and soldiers, to Carthage. Meanwhile, in Spain, where Hannibal's brother Hasdrubal remained with a large army in order to subjugate all of it for the Africans, Hasdrubal was defeated by the two Scipios, the Roman generals. In this battle, he lost thirty-five thousand men; ten thousand were captured, and twenty-five thousand were slain. The Carthaginians sent him twelve thousand infantry, four thousand cavalry, and twenty elephants to replenish his forces.

12. In the fourth year after Hannibal arrived in Italy, the consul Marcus Claudius Marcellus fought well against Hannibal at Nola, a city of Campania. Hannibal seized many Roman cities throughout Apulia, Calabria, and the land of the Brutii. Also at this time, King Philip of Macedonia sent delegates to Hannibal promising assistance, but under the condition that, after the Romans had been defeated, he in return would receive assistance from Hannibal against the Greeks. The Romans captured the delegates, and after their mission was revealed, they ordered Marcus Valerius Laevinius to go to Macedonia and Titus Manlius Torquatus to go to Sardinia as proconsul; for the Sardinians, incited by Hannibal, had deserted the Romans.

13. Thus, at the same time, war was waged in four places: in Italy against Hannibal, in Spain against his brother Hasdrubal, in Macedonia against Philip, and in Sardinia against the Sardinians and another Carthaginian named Hasdrubal. Hasdrubal was taken alive by the proconsul, Titus Manlius, who had been sent to Sardinia. Twelve thousand were slain, fifteen hundred were captured, and Sardinia was subjugated by the Romans. A victorious Manlius brought the captives and Hasdrubal back to Rome. Meanwhile, Philip was also defeated in Macedonia by Laevinius, as were Hasdrubal and Mago (the third brother of Hannibal) by the two Scipios in Spain.

14. In the tenth year after Hannibal's arrival in Italy, during the consulship of Publius Sulpicius and Cnaeus Fulvius, Hannibal came to the fourth milestone from the city, and his cavalry came all the way up to the gates. Soon, he retreated to Campania out of fear of the approaching consuls with the army. In Spain, both Scipios, who had been victorious for many years, were slain by Hannibal's brother

Hasdrubal; but their army remained unharmed, for they were taken by accident rather than in battle. At the same time, a large part of Sicily, which the Africans were beginning to take control of, was captured by the consul Marcellus, and an enormous amount of booty was brought to Rome from the renowned city of Syracuse. Laevinius made alliances with Philip in Macedonia, many Greek cities, and King Attalus of Asia. After setting out for Sicily, Laevinius captured a certain African general, Hanno, at Agrimentum, and captured the city itself as well. He sent Hanno and the captured nobles to Rome. He accepted the surrender of forty cities and stormed twenty-six others. After recovering all of Sicily and subduing Macedonia, Laevinius returned to Rome with great glory. In Italy, Hannibal attacked the consul Cnaeus Fulvius unexpectedly and killed him with eight thousand of his men.

15. Meanwhile, Publius Cornelius Scipio was sent to Spain, where there were no Roman generals after the two Scipios had been killed. He was twenty-four years old and the son of the same Publius Scipio who had waged war there before. He was regarded as first among the Romans, not only in his time, but in almost all later times as well. He captured New Carthage, where the Africans were keeping all of their gold, silver, and equipment of war, as well as the most noble hostages, which they had received from the Spaniards. He also captured Hannibal's brother Mago there, whom he sent to Rome with the others. There was great rejoicing in Rome after this was announced. Scipio returned all the hostages to their relatives; for which deed nearly all the Spaniards crossed over to his side in unison. After this, he sent Hasdrubal, the brother of Hannibal, fleeing and seized a great amount of booty.

16. Meanwhile, in Italy, Quintus Fabius Maximus recovered Tarentum, where large forces of Hannibal were stationed, and killed Hannibal's general, Karthalo, there as well. He sold at auction twenty-five thousand captives, distributed plunder to the soldiers, and returned the proceeds from the auctioned men to the public treasury. Then, many cities that formerly belonged to the Romans but had crossed over to Hannibal surrendered to Fabius Maximus. In Spain the following year, Scipio accomplished great things, both by himself and through his brother, Lucius Scipio, for they recovered seventy cities. In Italy, the Romans fought unsuccessfully, and the consul Claudius Marcellus was slain by Hannibal.

17. In the third year after Scipio set out for Spain, he again had notable achievements. After defeating a king of the Spaniards in a great battle, he made an alliance with him and became the first not to demand hostages from a defeated foe.

18. Hannibal, having lost hope that Spain could be held any longer against Scipio, summoned his brother Hasdrubal to Italy with all his forces. As Hasdrubal was traveling along the same route that Hannibal had taken, he fell into a trap placed by the consuls Appius Claudius Nero and Marcus Livius Salinator, near Sena, a city of Picenum, and died fighting bravely. A large number of his men were captured or slain, and a great amount of gold and silver was brought back to Rome. Hannibal began to despair about the outcome of the war after these events. The confidence of the Romans increased greatly, and they recalled Publius Cornelius Scipio from Spain. He arrived in Rome with great glory.

19. In the consulship of Quintus Caecilius and Lucius Valerius, all of the cities that Hannibal held in the land of the Bruttii surrendered to the Romans.

20. In the fourteenth year after Hannibal came to Italy, Scipio, who had accomplished much in Spain, was made consul and sent to Africa. It was thought that this man possessed a certain divine quality, so much so that it was believed that he held conversations with the gods. He fought in Africa against the African general Hanno and slaughtered his army. In a second battle, Scipio seized his camp, killed eleven thousand of his men, and captured four thousand five hundred. He captured Syphax, a king of Numidia who had joined with the Africans, and seized his camp. Syphax and the most noble of the Numidians were sent to Rome by Scipio along with vast plunder. Almost all of Italy deserted Hannibal after this was announced. Hannibal was ordered by the Carthaginians to return to Africa, which Scipio was laying waste.

21. Thus, Italy was freed from Hannibal in the seventeenth year. Carthaginian ambassadors sought peace from Scipio and were sent by him to the Senate in Rome. They were granted a truce of forty-five days, as long as it would take to travel to Rome and back, and thirty thousand pounds of silver were received from them. The Senate ordered peace to be made at the discretion of Scipio. Scipio offered these terms: they were not to keep more than thirty ships, they would pay five hundred thousand pounds of silver, and they would return Roman captives and fugitives.

22. Meanwhile, as Hannibal was arriving in Africa, the Africans committed many hostile acts, and the peace was broken. The ambassadors returning from Rome were captured but were released by the order of Scipio. Hannibal was defeated in a number of battles, and he himself sought peace from Scipio. When they met for a conference, the same terms were given as before but with an additional one hundred thousand pounds of silver added on account of the recent treachery. The Carthaginians were unhappy with the terms and ordered Hannibal to fight. Scipio and Masinissa, another king of the Numidians, who had allied with Scipio, brought the war to Carthage. Hannibal sent three scouts to the camp of Scipio. They were captured, and Scipio ordered for them to be led around the camp and to be shown the entire army. Then, Scipio had them fed and released in order for them to report to Hannibal what they had seen among the Romans.

23. Meanwhile, both generals prepared for a battle such as had almost never been seen before, since they were the most skilled men ever to lead forces to war. Scipio left victorious, almost capturing Hannibal, who at first escaped with many horsemen, then twenty, and finally, four. Twenty thousand pounds of silver, eighty pounds of gold, and an abundance of other goods were found in the camp of Hannibal. Peace was made with the Carthaginians after this battle. Scipio returned to Rome and celebrated a triumph with great glory. Henceforth, he was called "Africanus." Thus, the second Punic war ended nineteen years after it had begun.

Book IV

1. After the Punic war had ended, the Macedonian war against King Philip followed in the five hundred and fifty-first year after the founding of the city.

2. Titus Quintius Flaminius conducted the war successfully against Philip. Philip was granted peace under these conditions: he was not to attack those cities of Greece that the Romans had defended against him, he was to return the Roman prisoners and fugitives, he could keep only fifty ships and had to surrender the rest to the Romans, he was to pay four thousand pounds of silver per year for ten years, and he was to give his son Demetrius as a hostage. Titus Quintius also waged war against the Lacedaemonians. He defeated their general, Nabis, and received him into allegiance after imposing his own terms. In his triumph, he led with great glory before his chariot the most noble hostages, Demetrius, the son of Philip, and Armenes, the son of Nabis.

3. After the Macedonian war had ended, in the consulship of Publius Cornelius Scipio and Manius Acilius Glabrio, the Syrian war against King Antiochus began. Hannibal had joined Antiochus after fleeing his native Carthage out of fear that he would be handed over to the Romans. Manius Acilius Glabrio fought successfully in Achaia. The camp of King Antiochus was taken in a night battle, and the king himself was forced to flee. Since Philip had assisted the Romans against Antiochus, his son Demetrius was returned to him.

4. In the consulship of Lucius Cornelius Scipio and Caius Laelius,

Scipio Africanus set out against Antiochus as a lieutentant of his brother, Lucius Cornelius Scipio, the consul. Hannibal, who was with Antiochus, was defeated in a naval battle. Antiochus himself was routed by the consul Lucius Cornelius Scipio in a great battle at Magnesia, a city of Asia near Mt Sipylus. The Romans were assisted in this battle by Eumenes (who founded the city of Eumenia in Phrygia), the brother of King Attalus. Fifty thousand infantry and three thousand cavalry of King Antiochus were slain in this battle. The king then sought peace. Although he was now defeated, the same terms were offered by the Senate as before: he was to leave from Europe and Asia and stay near Mt. Taurus, he would pay ten thousand talents and provide twenty hostages, and he was to hand over Hannibal, the instigator of the war. All the cities of Asia that Antiochus had lost in the war were given by the Senate to King Eumenes. To the Rhodians, who had assisted the Romans against King Antiochus, many cities were granted. Lucius Cornelius Scipio returned to Rome and celebrated a triumph with great glory. He also received the name of "Asiaticus" in the same manner as his brother because he had conquered Asia, just as his brother was called "Africanus" on account of his having conquered Africa.

5. Marcus Fulvius held a triumph over the Aetolians during the consulship of Spurius Postumius Albinus and Quintus Marcius Philippus. Hannibal, in order not to be surrendered to the Romans after the defeat of Antiochus, fled to Prusias, the king of Bithnya. Titus Quintius Flaminius sought Hannibal from Prusias, and as Hannibal was about to be handed over to the Romans, he drank poison and was buried at Libyssa in the lands of the Nicomedians.

6. After Philip (the king of Macedonia who had waged war against the Romans and later assisted them against Antiochus) died, his son Perseus rebelled after preparing large forces for war. He had as allies Cotys, the king of Thrace, and Gentius, king of the Illyrians. The Romans had as allies Kings Eumenes of Asia, Ariaratus of Cappadocia, Antiochus of Syria, Ptolemy of Egypt, and Masinissa of Numidia. Although Prusias of Bithnya was married to Perseus' sister, he remained neutral. The consul Publius Licinius was sent against him as the Roman general and was defeated by the king in a fierce battle. Although the Romans had been defeated, they refused to grant peace to the king seeking it except under the following condition: he was to surrender himself and his people to the Roman Senate and people. The consul Lucius Aemilius Paulus was sent against him, and the praetor Caius Anicius was sent against Gentius in Illyricum. Gentius was easily defeated in one battle, and soon after, surrendered himself. His mother, wife, two sons, and brother fell into the power of the Romans at the same time. Thus, the war was ended within thirty days, and it was learned that Gentius was defeated before it was announced that the war had begun.

7. The consul Aemilius Paulus fought Perseus and defeated him on September 3rd, killing twenty thousand of his infantry. The cavalry fled unharmed with the king, and the Romans lost one hundred soldiers. All the cities of Macedonia under the king's control surrendered themselves to the Romans. The king himself, having been deserted by his friends, fell into the power of the consul Aemilius Paulus, but Paulus did not treat him at all as if he had been defeated. He did not allow Perseus to grovel at his feet, and he placed him on a seat beside himself. The Romans gave the Macedonians and Illyrians the following terms: they would remain free, and they would only pay half the amount of tribute that they had paid to the kings, in order for it to be seen that the Romans fight more out of a sense of justice than out of greed. Paulus announced these terms to a vast assembly of people and then, in a magnificent feast, fed the delegates who had come to him from many nations, saying that "a man should be able to both conquer in war and be elegant in laying out a feast."

8. Soon, Paulus captured seventy cities of Epirus which were rebelling and distributed the booty to his soldiers. He returned to Rome with great pomp in Perseus' ship, which was said to be of such extraordinary size that it was reported to have had sixteen rows of oars. He celebrated a magnificent triumph in a gold chariot with his two sons standing on either side. King Perseus himself, aged forty-five, was led before the chariot with his two sons. After Paulus, Anicius celebrated a triumph over the Illyrians. Gentius was led with his brother and sons before the chariot. The kings of many nations came to Rome to see this spectacle, including Attalus and Eumenes, kings of Asia, among others, and Prusias of Bithnya. They were welcomed with great honor, and with the permission of the Senate, they placed gifts that they had brought with them in the Capitol. Additionally, Prusias entrusted his son Nicomedes to the Senate.

9. In the following year, Lucius Memmius fought well in Lusitania. Marcellus, the succeeding consul, managed affairs successfully in the same country.

10. A third war against Carthage was then undertaken in the six hundred and second year since the founding of the city, during the consulship of Lucius Manlius Censorinus and Manius Manilius, in the fifty-first year after the second Punic war had ended. After setting out, the consuls attacked Carthage. Hasdrubal, the Carthaginian general, fought against them. Another general, Famea, was in charge of the Carthaginian cavalry. At this time, Scipio, the grandson of Scipio Africanus, was serving as a tribune. Everyone had great fear and respect for him, for he was considered the most skilled and experienced in warfare. The consuls had much success through Scipio, and there was nothing that either Hasdrubal or Famea feared more than to join in battle against the Romans where Scipio was fighting.

11. Around the same time, Masinissa, king of the Numidians and ally of the Roman people for almost sixty years, died at ninety-seven years of age, leaving behind forty-four sons. He designated Scipio as the one to divide his kingdom amongst his sons.

12. Therefore, since the name of Scipio was already famous, he was made consul, although still a young man, and was sent against Carthage. Scipio captured and demolished the city. Plunder, which the Africans had collected from the destruction of various cities, was found there. Scipio returned ornaments to the cities of Sicily, Italy, and Africa which they recognized as belonging to them. Thus, Carthage was destroyed in the seven hundredth year after it was founded. Scipio earned the name that his grandfather had received, and indeed, on account of his valor, was called "Africanus the

Younger."

13. Meanwhile, in Macedonia, a certain Pseudophilippus took up arms and defeated Publius Iuventius, the Roman praetor who had been sent against him, in a great massacre. Next, Quintus Caecilius Metullus was sent as general by the Romans against Pseudophilippus. After slaying twenty-five thousand of his men, Metellus recovered Macedonia and brought Pseudophilippus under his control.

14. War was declared against Corinth, the noblest city of Greece, because of injuries to some Roman ambassadors. The consul Mummius captured the city and destroyed it. Therefore, three great triumphs were held simultaneously in Rome: the triumph of Africanus for Africa, in which Hasdrubal was led before his chariot; the triumph of Metellus for Macedonia, whose chariot Andriscus, also known as Pseudophilippus, preceded; and the triumph of Mummius for Corinth, before whom bronze statues, painted tablets, and other ornaments of that most famous city were carried.

15. In another revolt in Macedonia, Pseudoperses, who claimed to be the son of Perseus, gathered a group of slaves and rebelled. When he had sixteen thousand of them under arms, he was defeated by Tremellius, the quaestor.

16. At the same time, Metellus achieved great success in Celtiberia among the Spaniards. Quintus Pompeius succeeded him. Quintus Caepio was sent to the same war, which a certain Viriathus was conducting in Lusitania. Fearing this, Viriathus' own men killed him. He had stirred up Spain against the Romans for fourteen years. Viriathus had started out as a shepherd, then he was the leader of a group of thieves, and finally, he incited so many people to war that he was regarded as the protector of Spain against the Romans. When his assassins went to the consul Caepio to seek a reward, they received a reply that it was never pleasing to the Romans to have a general slain by his own soldiers.

17. Afterwards, Quintus Pompeius, the consul, was defeated and arranged a contemptible peace with the Numantians, who possessed the most powerful city in Spain. The consul Caius Hostilius Mancinus also arranged a disgraceful peace with the Numantians after him. The Roman people and Senate ordered this treaty to be broken and Mancinus to be handed over to the enemy in order for him, as the author of the treaty, to be the one that the Numantians punished for violating it. Therefore, after the great embarrassment of the Roman army being beaten twice by the Numantians, Publius Scipio Africanus was made consul for the second time and was sent to Numantia. Scipio first reformed the disorderly and idle soldiers through training rather than by punishment, and without resorting to severity; then he took many Spanish cities, capturing some and accepting the surrender of others. Finally, he starved Numantia itself into submission after a long siege and leveled it to the ground. He then received the allegiance of the rest of the province.

18. At that same time, Attalus, king of Asia and brother of Eumenes, died and left the Roman people as his heir. Thus, Asia was added to the Roman Empire by a will.

19. Shortly afterwards, Decimus Junius Brutus celebrated a triumph with great glory over the Callaeci and Lusitanians, and Publius Scipio Africanus celebrated his second triumph, over the Numantians, fourteen years after he had celebrated one for Africa.

20. In the meantime, Aristonicus, the son of Eumenes from a concubine, started a war in Asia. This Eumenes was the brother of Attalus. Publius Licinius Crassus was sent against Aristonicus. He received great assistance from several kings. Kings Nicomedes of Bithnya, Mithridates of Pontus (with whom afterwards the Romans fought a very serious war), Ariarathes of Cappadocia, and Pylaemenes of Paphlagonia all aided the Romans. Nevertheless, Crassus was defeated and slain in battle. His head was brought to Aristonicus, and his body was buried at Smyrna. Perperna, the Roman consul who was coming to succeed Crassus, hurried into Asia upon hearing of the outcome of the battle. He defeated Aristonicus near Stratonice, the city where Aristonicus had fled to, and compelled him to surrender from hunger. Aristonicus was strangled in prison in

Rome by order of the Senate, for a triumph could not be held concerning him because Perperna had died near Pergamum while returning to Rome.

21. In the consulship of Lucius Caecilius Metellus and Titus Quintius Flamininus, Carthage was rebuilt in Africa by order of the Senate, twenty-two years after it had been demolished by Scipio, and Roman citizens were brought there as colonists. This city still exists today.

22. In the six hundred and twenty-seventh year since the founding of the city, the consuls Caius Cassius Longinus and Sextus Domitius Calvinus waged war against the transalpine Gauls, the city of the Arverni (which was quite renowned at that time), and the Arvernian leader, Bituitus. The consuls killed great numbers of them near the river Rhone and carried a vast amount of plunder from the torques of the Gauls back to Rome. Bituitus surrendered to Domitius and was brought by him to Rome. Both consuls triumphed with great glory.

23. During the consulship of Marcus Porcius Cato and Quintus Marcius Rex, in the six hundred and thirty-third year since the founding of the city, a colony was established at Narbo in Gaul. A year later, a triumph was celebrated by the consuls Lucius Caecilius Metellus and Quintus Mucius Scaevola over Dalmatia.

24. In the six hundred and thirty-fifth year after the city was founded, the consul Caius Cato went to war against the Scordisci and fought disgracefully.

25. In the consulship of Caius Caecilius Metellus and Cnaeus Carbo, the two Metellus brothers celebrated triumphs, one for Sardinia and the other for Thrace, on the same day, and it was announced in Rome that the Cimbri had entered Italy from Gaul.

26. During the consulship of Publius Scipio Nasica and Lucius Calpurnius Bestia, war was waged against Jugurtha, king of the Numidians, because he had killed his brothers, Adherbal and Hiempsal, who were the sons of Micipsa as well as kings and friends of the Roman people. The consul Calpurnius Bestia was sent out against him, but he was corrupted by the money of the king and arranged a disgraceful peace with him. This was rejected by the Senate. The next year, Spurius Postumius Albinus set out against Jugurtha. He also, through the agency of his brother, fought dishonorably against the Numidians.

27. A third consul, Quintus Caecilius Metellus, was sent against Jugurtha. He restored Roman discipline to the army by using harsh measures and strict guidance, while not resorting to cruelty. He defeated Jugurtha in various battles, killed or captured his elephants, and took many of his cities. When he was about to end the war, he was succeeded by Caius Marius. Marius defeated both Jugurtha and Bocchus, a king of Mauritania who had begun to assist Jugurtha. He also took several cities of Numidia and put an end to the war by capturing Jugurtha by means of his quaestor, Cornelius Sulla, a remarkable man. Jugurtha was betrayed by Bocchus, who had earlier fought on his behalf. Marcus Junius Silanus, the colleague of Quintus Metellus, defeated the Cimbri in Gaul, Minucius Rufus defeated the Scordisci and Triballi in Macedonia, and Servilius Caepio defeated the Lusitani in Spain. Two triumphs were celebrated in regards to Jugurtha; the first by Metellus and the second by Marius. However, it was before the chariot of Marius that Jugurtha was led in chains with his two sons, and soon afterwards, he was strangled in prison by order of the consul.

Book V

1. While the war in Numidia was being waged against Jugurtha, the Roman consuls Marcus Manlius and Quintus Caepio were defeated near the river Rhone by the Cimbri, Teutons, Tigurini, and Ambrones, who were Germanic and Gallic tribes. They also lost their camp and a large part of their army in a great slaughter. There was great fear in Rome, almost as great as during the Punic war in the time of Hannibal, that the Gauls would again come to Rome. Therefore, Marius, after his victory over Jugurtha, was made consul for the second time, and the management of the war against the Cimbri and Teutons was decreed to him. He was granted third and fourth consulships because the Cimbrian war dragged on. In his fourth consulship, he had a colleague, Quintus Lutatius Catalus. Thus, Marius fought against the Cimbri, and in two battles, killed two hundred thousand of the enemy and captured eighty thousand with their leader, Teutobodus. Marius was made consul for a fifth time, although he was not present, on account of this service.

2. Meanwhile, the Teutons and Cimbri, of whom there were still vast numbers, crossed into Italy. Caius Marius and Quintus Catalus again fought against them, with Catulus enjoying the greater success; for in the battle which both consuls conducted, one hundred and forty thousand were slaughtered, either in the battle or in flight, and sixty thousand were captured. Three hundred soldiers died from both Roman armies. Thirty-three military standards of the Cimbri were carried off; two by Marius' army and thirty-one by Catulus'. This was the end of the war. A triumph was decreed for each of them.

3. During the consulship of Sextus Julius Caesar and Lucius Marcius Philippus, in the six hundred and fifty-ninth year since the founding of the city, when almost all other wars had ceased, the Picentes, Marsi, and Peligni started a very serious war. Although they had been subservient to the Romans for many years, they began to claim equal liberty for themselves. This was a very destructive war. Publius Rutilius — the consul, Caepio — a young nobleman, and Porcius Cato — another consul, were slain in it. The Picentes and Marsi had as generals against the Romans, Titus Vettius, Hierius Asinius, Titus Herennius, and Aulus Cluentius. The Romans Caius Marius (the six-time consul), Cnaeus Pompey, and particularly Lucius Cornelius Sulla, fought well. Among other outstanding accomplishments, Sulla routed Cluentius, the enemy general, and his numerous forces, while only losing one of his own men. The war dragged on for four years with great loss. Finally, in the fifth year, the war was ended by Lucius Cornelius Sulla, the consul, who earlier in the same war, as a praetor, had energetically accomplished many things.

4. In the six hundred and sixty-second year since the founding of the city, the first civil war flared up at Rome, and also in the same year, the Mithridatic war began. Caius Marius, the six-time consul, provided the cause for the civil war. For after Sulla, the consul, was assigned the war against Mithridates (who had seized Asia and Achaia), and while he was staying a short time in Campania in order to clean up the remnants of the aforementioned Social war waged in Italy, Marius arranged for his own assignment to the Mithridatic war. Angered by this, Sulla came to the city with the army and fought there against Marius and Sulpicius. He was the first general to enter the city of Rome in arms. He killed Sulpicius, forced Marius to flee, and after selecting Cnaeus Octavius and Lucius Cornelius Cinna as consuls for the coming year, he set out for Asia.

5. For Mithridates (the king of Pontus, who also held Lesser Armenia and the entire circuit of the Pontic sea with the Bosposrus) wished to expel Nicomedes, a friend of the Roman people, from Bithnya, and declared to the Senate that he would wage war against Nicomedes on account of injuries he had suffered. The Senate replied to Mithridates that if he should do this, he too would suffer war from the Romans.

Angry over this, he immediately seized Cappadocia and forced Ariobarzanes, king and friend of the Roman people, to flee. Soon, he also invaded Bithnya and Paphlagonia, routing kings Pylaemenes and Nicomedes, friends of the Roman people. From there, he hastened to Ephesus and sent letters throughout Asia, directing that wherever Roman citizens were found, they should be killed the same day.

6. Meanwhile, Athens, a city of Achaia, was handed over to Mithridates by Aristion, an Athenian; for Mithridates had already sent Archelaus, his general, to Achaia with one hundred and twenty thousand cavalry and infantry, and he occupied the rest of Greece. Sulla besieged Archelaus at Piraeus, not far from Athens, and captured Athens itself. Afterwards, Sulla joined battle with Archelaus and defeated him so thoroughly that scarcely ten thousand out of one hundred and twenty thousand of Archelaus' men survived, while Sulla lost only thirteen men. Mithridates, after hearing of the battle, sent seventy thousand picked men from Asia to Archelaus, and he and Sulla met in battle again. In the first encounter, fifteen thousand of the enemy and Diogenes, the son of Archelaus, were slain. In the second battle, all the forces of Mithridates were wiped out, and Archelaus himself hid unarmed for three days in a swamp. When Mithridates heard what had happened, he ordered for peace to be negotiated with Sulla.

7. In the meantime, Sulla defeated some of the Dardani, Scordisci, Dalmatians, and Maedi, and received the rest in allegiance. When representatives came from Mithridates seeking peace, Sulla responded that he would only grant peace if the king left the lands he had seized and returned to his kingdom. Nevertheless, they both met for a conference afterwards. Peace was arranged between them so that Sulla, as he was hastening to the civil war, would not have an enemy at his back; for while Sulla was defeating Mithridates in Achaia and Asia, Marius, who had been forced to flee, and Cornelius Cinna, one of the consuls, had renewed the war in Italy and entered the city of Rome. They killed the noblest men of the Senate and men of consular rank. They proscribed many. They demolished the house of Sulla himself and forced his wife and sons to flee. The remainder of the Senate came fleeing from the city to Sulla in Greece and begged him to come to the aid of his country. Sulla crossed over into Italy to wage war against the consuls, Norbanus and Scipio. In the first battle, he fought against Norbanus, not far from Capua. Sulla killed six thousand of Norbanus' men, captured six thousand, and lost one hundred and twenty-four of his own. Then he turned to Scipio, and before the battle or any bloodshed, he accepted the surrender of his whole army.

8. When the consuls changed in Rome, Marius, the son of Marius, and Papirius Carbo received the consulship. Sulla fought against the younger Marius, killing fifteen thousand of Marius' men while only losing four hundred of his own. Soon afterwards, Sulla also entered the city. He besieged the younger Marius at Praeneste, after pursuing him there, and compelled him to commit suicide. He fought another fierce battle, against Lamponius and Carinas, generals of the Marian faction, near the Collina gate. There were said to have been seventy thousand of the enemy in this battle against Sulla. Twelve thousand surrendered to Sulla, the rest were consumed in the battle, in the camp, and in flight, by the insatiable anger of the victors. In addition, Cnaeus Carbo, the other consul, fled from Ariminum to Sicily and was slain there by Cnaeus Pompey. After learning of his diligence, Sulla put Pompey, a young man of twenty-one, in charge of the surrendered armies, so that he was regarded as second only to Sulla himself.

9. Therefore, Pompey recovered Sicily after slaying Carbo. From there, he crossed over to Africa and killed Domitius, a general of the Marian faction, and Hiarbas, the king of Mauritania who was aiding Domitius. After these events, Sulla celebrated a glorious triumph over Mithridates. Also, Cnaeus Pompey, at twenty-four years of age, celebrated a triumph over Africa. No Roman had ever been granted a triumph at that age before. This was the end of two very destructive wars: the Italian, which was also called the Social war, and the civil war; both of which had dragged on for ten years. More than one hundred and fifty thousand men — twenty-four of consular rank, seven of praetorian, sixty of aedilitian, and almost two hundred senators perished.

Book VI

1. In the consulship of Marcus Aemilius Lepidus and Quintus Catulus, after Sulla had settled the affairs of the republic, new wars flared up; one in Spain, another in Pamphylia and Cilicia, a third in Macedonia, and a fourth in Dalmatia. Sertorius, who had belonged to the Marian faction, feared the fate of the others who had been slain and incited Spain to war. The generals sent against him were Quintus Caecilius Metellus, the son of Metellus who had defeated King Jugurtha, and Lucius Domitius, the praetor. Domitius was slain by Sertorius' general, Hirtuleius. Metellus fought against Sertorius with mixed success. Afterwards, since Metellus by himself was thought to be unequal to the challenge, Cnaeus Pompey was sent to Spain. Sertorius fought often with varied success against the two opposing generals. Finally, in the eighth year, Sertorius was slain by his own men, and the young Cnaeus Pompey and Quintus Metellus Pius ended the war. Almost all of Spain was brought under the authority of the Roman people.

2. Appius Claudius was sent to Macedonia after his consulship. He fought several minor engagements against various tribes inhabiting the province of Rhodopa and died there from illness. After his consulship, Caius Scribonius Curio was sent there as his successor. He defeated the Dardani, advancing all the way to the Danube, and earned a triumph, having ended the war inside of three years.

3. Publius Servilius, a vigorous man, was sent to Cilicia and Pamphylia after his consulship. He subjugated Cilicia and stormed and captured the most famous cities of Lycia, among which were

Phaselis, Olympus, and Corycus. He also attacked the Isaurians and brought them under Roman control. He finished the war within three years and was the first of all the Romans to march in the Taurus mountains. On his return, he received a triumph and obtained the name "Isauricus."

4. Caius Cosconius was sent to Illyricum as proconsul. He subjugated a large part of Dalmatia, captured Salonae, and having ended the war, he returned two years after he had left.

5. Around the same time, the consul Marcus Aemilius Lepidus, the colleague of Catulus, attempted to incite a civil war, but in the space of one summer, his uprising was crushed. Thus, there were many triumphs at the same time; Metellus' for Spain, Pompey's second (also for Spain), Curio's for Macedonia, and Servilius' for Isauria.

6. In the six hundred and seventy-sixth year after the city's founding, when Lucius Licinius Lucullus and Marcus Aurelius Cotta were consuls, Nicomedes, the king of Bithnya, died and left the Roman people as heir in his will. Mithridates disrupted the peace and again attempted to invade Bithnya and Asia. Both consuls were sent against him with mixed success. Cotta was defeated in battle by him near Chalcedon, and was forced into the town and besieged. But when Mithridates left from there to Cyzicus, in order to invade Asia after Cyzicus was captured, Lucullus came upon him. While Mithridates lingered in the siege of Cyzicus, Lucullus besieged him from the rear, wore him out from hunger, and defeated him in many battles. Finally, he forced him to flee to Byzantium, which is now Constantinople. Lucullus defeated his commanders in a naval battle as well. Thus, in a single winter and summer, up to one hundred thousand of the king's men were slain by Lucullus.

7. In the city of Rome's six hundred and seventy-eighth year, Marcus Licinius Lucullus, the cousin of Lucullus who had waged war against Mithridates, obtained the province of Macedonia; and in Italy, a new war suddenly flared up. Seventy-four gladiators, led by Spartacus, Crixus, and Oenomaus, broke out of their gladiator school at Capua and fled. As they roamed through Italy, they started a war that was not much less serious than that of Hannibal. After they had defeated several generals and both consuls at once, and raised an army of some sixty thousand armed men, they were defeated by the proconsul, Marcus Licinius Crassus, in Apulia. This war was ended in the third year after many calamities to Italy.

8. In the six hundred and eighty-first year since the founding of the city, in the consulship of Publius Cornelius Lentulus and Cnaeus Aufidius Orestes, there were only two serious wars in the Roman Empire — the Mithridatic and Macedonian. The two Luculli, Lucius Lucullus and Marcus Lucullus, were conducting these wars. After the battle at Cyzicus, in which Lucius Lucullus defeated Mithridates, and the naval battle in which he defeated his commanders, Lucius Lucullus pursued Mithridates and recovered Paphlagonia and Bithnya. He also invaded his kingdom and captured Sinope and Amisus, the noblest cities of Pontus. In a second battle near the city of Cabira, where Mithridates had brought an enormous number of men from his entire kingdom, thirty thousand select troops of the king were annihilated by five thousand Romans. Mithridates was forced to flee, and his camp was seized. Lesser Armenia, which Mithridates held, was taken from him as well. Mithridates was given refuge by Tigranes, the king of Armenia, who at that time reigned in great glory. Tigranes had defeated the Persians often and seized Mesopotamia, Syria, and part of Phoenicia.

9. Therefore, Lucullus, as he was pursuing the fleeing enemy, also entered the kingdom of Tigranes, who ruled the Armenias. He captured Tigranocerta, a city of Arzanena, the most noble of the Armenian kingdom. With eighteen thousand soldiers, he defeated the king himself, who was approaching with seven thousand five hundred cuirassiers and one hundred thousand archers and armed men, destroying a large part of the Armenians in the process. From there, he proceeded to Nisbis and captured that city as well, along with the brother of the king. But those whom Lucullus left in Pontus with part of the army for the sake of guarding the regions that the Romans had already conquered, gave another chance to Mithridates, through negligence and greed, of invading Pontus, and thus the war was renewed. After Nisbis was captured, while Lucullus was preparing an expedition against the Persians, a successor was sent to him.

10. The other Lucullus, who was managing affairs in Macedonia, was the first of the Romans to wage war against the Bessi and defeated them in a great battle on Mount Haemus. He took the town of Uscudama, which the Bessi were inhabiting, on the same day that he attacked it. He captured Cabyle and penetrated all the way to the Danube. He went on from there and attacked many cities located above Pontus. There he destroyed Apollonia and captured Callatis, Parthenopolis, Tomis, Histrus, and Berziaone. Then, having ended the war, he returned to Rome. Both Luculli celebrated triumphs, but with the one who had fought against Mithridates enjoying the greater glory since he had returned victorious over such great kingdoms.

11. When the Macedonian war was finished, but the Mithridatic war (which the king had renewed after gathering his forces when Lucullus departed) still remained, the Cretan war arose. Quintus Caecilius Metellus was sent to the Cretan war, and he captured the whole province within three years in a series of great battles. He was given the name "Creticus," and he celebrated a triumph over that island. At this time, Libya was also added to the Roman Empire, through the will of Appion, its king. In it were the renowned cities of Berenice, Ptolomais, and Cyrene.

12. While these events were taking place, pirates were infesting all the seas. Since the Romans were victorious throughout the world, only travel at sea was not safe. Therefore, the war against the pirates was decreed to Cnaeus Pompey. He finished the war with great haste and good fortune within a few months. Soon, he was also given the war against Kings Mithridates and Tigranes. After undertaking the war, he defeated Mithridates in Lesser Armenia in a night battle, seizing his camp and killing forty thousand of his men, while losing only twenty men and two centurions from his own army. Mithridates fled with his wife and two companions. Not much afterwards, when he was raging at his own men, he was forced to commit suicide by the revolt of his son, Pharnaces, along with the soldiers, and he drank poison. This was the end of Mithridates, a man of great energy and prudence. He died near the Bosporus. He had reigned for sixty years, lived for seventy-two, and was at war with the Romans for forty.

13. Then, Pompey waged war against Tigranes. Tigranes surrendered to Pompey and came to his camp, located at the sixteenth milestone from Artaxta. As he was prostrating himself at the knees of Pompey, he placed his diadem in Pompey's hands. Pompey returned his diadem to him and treated him honorably, but fined him part of his kingdom and a large amount of money. Syria, Phoenicia, and Sophene were taken from him, and he was ordered to pay six thousand silver talents to the Roman people because he had waged war against them without cause.

14. Soon, Pompey also waged war against the Albani and defeated their king, Orodes, three times. Finally, after peace was sought through letters and gifts, Pompey granted a pardon and peace to Orodes. He also defeated Artoces, the king of Iberia [Eastern Iberia], in battle and accepted his surrender. He gave lesser Armenia to Deiotarus, king of Galatia, because he had been an ally in the Mithridatic war. He returned Paphlagonia to Attalus and Pylaemenes, and imposed Aristarchus as king of Colchis. Soon after, he defeated the Itureans and Arabians. When he arrived in Syria, he gave Seleucia, a city near Antioch, its liberty because it had not admitted King Tigranes. He returned their hostages to the people of Antioch. He gave a considerable amount of land to the Daphnians, in order for them to expand their sacred grove, after being delighted by the pleasantness of the place and the abundance of the waters there. From there he went to Judea and captured Jerusalem, the capital of that nation, in three months, while slaying twelve thousand Jews and receiving the rest in allegiance. After these deeds, he returned to Asia and put an end to the Romans' longest war.

15. In the consulship of Marcus Tullius Cicero, the orator, and Caius Antonius, in the six hundred and eighty-ninth year since the founding of the city, Lucius Sergius Catalina, a man of the highest birth but of very depraved character, conspired to destroy the state with certain distinguished, but rash, men. He was expelled from the city by Cicero, and his co-conspirators were arrested and strangled in prison.

Catalina himself was defeated in battle and slain by the other consul, Antonius.

16. In the six hundred and ninetieth year from the founding of the city, in the consulship of Decimus Junius Silanus and Lucius Murena, Metellus triumphed for Crete, and Pompey triumphed for the pirate and Mithridatic wars. There has never been a triumph equal in ostentation to Pompey's. The sons of Mithridates, the son of Tigranes, and Aristobulus, king of the Jews, were led before his chariot. A colossal sum of money and an immense weight of gold and silver were carried before his chariot. At this time, there were no serious wars throughout the world.

17. In the six hundred and ninety-third year since the city's founding, Caius Julius Caesar, who reigned afterwards, was made consul with Lucius Bibulus. Gaul and Illyricum were decreed to him with ten legions. First, he defeated the Helvetii, who are now called the Sequani; then, he proceeded all the way to the British ocean by conquering in great wars. In nine years, he subdued almost all of Gaul, which lies between the Alps, the river Rhone, the river Rhine, and the ocean — a circuit of three thousand two hundred miles. He soon brought war to the Britons, who had not even heard of the name of the Romans before him. He defeated them as well, and after receiving hostages from them, he made them pay tribute. He demanded from Gaul, in the name of tribute, forty million sesterces a year. After advancing against the Germans across the Rhine, he defeated them in a number of savage battles. Among so many successes, he was unsuccessful in battle three times — once among the Arverni while present, and twice in Germany while absent; for two of his lieutenants, Titurius and Aurunculeius, were slain by treachery.

18. Around the same time, in the six hundred and ninety-seventh year since the founding of the city, Marcus Licinius Crassus, the colleague of Cnaeus Pompey the Great in his second consulship, was sent against the Parthians. After entering battle near Carrhae, contrary to the omens and auspices, he was defeated by Surena, a general of King Orodes, and was ultimately slain with his son, an illustrious and distinguished young man. The rest of the army was saved by Caius Cassius, who restored the situation with singular courage and such great valor that, as they were retreating across the Euphrates, he defeated the Persians in numerous battles.

19. Henceforth, an execrable and lamentable civil war followed, and in addition to the calamities they suffered in battle, the fortune of the Roman people was changed as well. For when Caesar was returning victorious from Gaul, he began to demand another consulship and that it be granted to him without delay. This was opposed by the consul Marcellus, Bibulus, Pompey, and Cato, and Caesar was ordered to dismiss his armies and return to the city. Due to this insult, he departed from Ariminum, where his soldiers were assembled, and marched with the army against his country. The consuls, along with Pompey, the entire Senate, and all the nobility, fled from the city and crossed over into Greece. The Senate, with Pompey as general, prepared for war against Caesar in Epirus, Macedonia, and Achaia.

20. Caesar entered the vacated city and made himself dictator. From there he headed to Spain. There, he defeated three powerful and brave armies of Pompey with their generals — Lucius Afranius, Marcus Petreius, and Marcus Varro. After returning from there, he crossed into Greece and fought against Pompey. In the first battle, Caesar was defeated and routed but escaped because night was intervening, and Pompey was unwilling to pursue him. Caesar remarked that Pompey did not know how to conquer and that Pompey could have vanquished him on that day alone. Next, near Paleopharsulus in Thessaly, they both fought after leading forth great numbers of men. The line of Pompey had forty thousand infantry, six hundred horsemen on the left wing, five hundred on the right, auxiliary troops from all of the East, the entire nobility, innumerable senators, men of praetorian and consular rank, and men who had already been victorious in great wars. Caesar had not quite thirty thousand infantry in his line and a thousand horsemen.

21. Never before had Roman forces convened in one place in greater numbers or under more skilled leaders. They could have easily subjugated the entire world if only they had been led against the barbarians. The battle was fought with great contention, but at last, Pompey was defeated, and his camp was taken. Pompey himself fled to Alexandria in order to seek assistance from the king of Egypt, whom Pompey had been appointed guardian over by the Senate on account of his young age. The king, pursuing fortune rather than friendship, killed Pompey and sent his head and ring to Caesar; at the sight of which, even Caesar is said to have wept as he gazed at the head of so great a man, who was also once his son-in-law.

22. Caesar soon arrived in Alexandria. Ptolemy planned a trap for him also, and because of this, war was waged against him as well. Ptolemy perished in the Nile after being defeated, and his body was found wearing golden armor. Caesar took control of Alexandria and gave the kingdom to Cleopatra, with whom he was having an affair and who was also the sister of Ptolemy. As he was returning from there, Caesar defeated in battle the son of Mithridates the Great, Pharnaces, who had aided Pompey in Thessaly and revolted in Pontus, occupying many provinces of the Roman people. Afterwards, Caesar compelled him to commit suicide.

23. Upon returning from there to Rome, Caesar made himself consul for the third time, with Marcus Aemilius Lepidus, who had been the master of horse to him as dictator the preceding year. Then, he set out for Africa where a great multitude of the nobility with King Juba, the king of Mauritania, were renewing the war. The Roman leaders were Publius Cornelius Scipio (also the father-in-law of Pompey) of the ancient family of Scipio Africanus, Marcus Petreius, Quintus Varus, Marcus Porcius Cato, and Lucius Cornelius Faustus, the son of the dictator Sulla. Caesar entered battle against them, and after many struggles, was victorious. Cato, Scipio, Petreius, and Juba killed themselves. Faustus, son of the former dictator Sulla and son-in-law of Pompey, was slain by Caesar.

24. Caesar returned to Rome the next year and made himself consul for the fourth time. He departed at once for Spain, where the sons of Pompey, Cnaeus Pompey and Sextus Pompey, had prepared a vast war. There were many battles, the last of which was near the city of Munda, where Caesar was so close to being beaten that, as his men were beginning to flee, he was planning to commit suicide in order not to fall, at fifty-six years of age, into the power of young men after such great military glory. His men rallied at last, and he was victorious. Of the sons of Pompey, the elder was slain and the younger fled.

25. Then, after the civil wars were finished throughout the world, Caesar returned to Rome. He began to act more arrogantly and contrary to the custom of Roman liberty. Therefore, when he bestowed honors which previously were conferred by the people, failed to rise as the Senate approached him, and did other things in a kingly and almost tyrannical fashion, a conspiracy was formed against him by sixty or more Roman senators and knights. Chief among the conspirators were the two Bruti (from the family of Brutus who was the first consul of Rome and who had expelled the kings), Caius Cassius, and Servilius Casca. When he went to the senate house with the others on the day of the convening of the Senate, he was stabbed twenty-three times.

Book VII

1. In about the seven hundred and ninth year of the city, after Caesar had been slain, the civil wars resumed; for the Senate favored the assassins of Caesar, while Antony, the consul and a member of Caesar's faction, was attempting to crush them in a civil war. Therefore, since the republic was now in turmoil, Antony, who was committing many offenses, was judged an enemy by the Senate. The two consuls, Pansa and Hirtius, and Octavian (a young man of eighteen, the nephew of Caesar whom he had left as heir in his will and ordered to bear his name) were sent to pursue him. This is the man who, afterwards, was called Augustus and took over the government. These three generals set out and defeated Antony. However, it came about that both victorious consuls died; therefore, the three armies came under the authority of Caesar Augustus alone.

2. After being defeated and losing his army, Antony fled and was given refuge by Lepidus, who had been Caesar's master of horse and was in possession of strong forces at this time. Soon, through the efforts of Lepidus, Caesar made peace with Antony and set out with the army for Rome as though he was going to avenge the death of his father (who had adopted him in his will). He forcibly obtained the consulship at twenty years of age. He proscribed the Senate, and with Antony and Lepidus, began to rule the republic by arms. Through the agency of these men, Cicero the orator was slain, as well as many other nobles.

3. Meanwhile, Brutus and Cassius, the assassins of Caesar, started a great war, for there were many armies throughout Macedonia and the

East that they had seized. Therefore, Caesar Octavian Augustus and Mark Antony set out against them while Lepidus remained to defend Italy. They fought against them near Philippi, a city of Macedonia. In the first battle, Antony and Caesar were defeated, however, Cassius, the leader of the nobility, perished. In the second battle, they defeated and killed Brutus and a vast number of the nobility who had waged war with him. Thus, the republic was divided between them, with Augustus taking Spain, Gaul, and Italy, and Antony taking Asia, Pontus, and the East; but in Italy, Lucius Antony, the consul and brother of Antony who fought with Caesar against Brutus and Cassius, sparked a civil war. He was defeated and captured near Perusia, a city of Tuscia, but was not slain.

4. In the meantime, Sextus Pompey, the son of Cnaeus Pompey the Great, incited a serious war in Sicily after the survivors from the faction of Brutus and Cassius joined him. Caesar Augustus Octavian and Mark Antony waged war against him. At last, peace was agreed upon.

5. During this time, Marcus Agrippa managed affairs successfully in Lusitania, and Lucius Ventidius Bassus defeated the Persians in three battles while they were invading Syria. He killed Pacorus, son of King Orodes of Persia, on the very same day on which Orodes had once killed Crassus through the agency of his general Surena. He was the first to celebrate a legitimate triumph over the Parthians in Rome.

6. Meanwhile, Pompey disrupted the peace and was defeated in a naval battle. He was slain while fleeing to Asia. Antony, who possessed Asia and the East, divorced the sister of Caesar Augustus Octavian and married Queen Cleopatra of Egypt. He also fought against the Persians. He defeated them in the first few battles, however, as he was returning, he struggled with hunger and pestilence, and since the Parthians were pressing him as he retreated, he fled as though he had been defeated.

7. Antony also started a major civil war, compelled by his wife Cleopatra, the queen of Egypt who longed with womanly desire to reign in the city as well. He was defeated in a famous and renowned naval battle near Actium, located in Epirus. He fled from there to Egypt, and perceiving his situation as hopeless since all his men were switching allegiance to Augustus, he took his own life. Cleopatra held an asp to herself and perished from its venom. Through Augustus, Egypt was added to the Roman Empire, and Caius Cornelius Gallus was placed in charge of it. This man was the first Roman judge Egypt had.

8. Thus, with all the civil wars completed throughout the world, Octavian Augustus returned to Rome in the twelfth year after he had been made consul. From this time on, he ruled the state alone for forty-four years. Earlier, he had ruled for twelve years with Antony and Lepidus. Thus, his reign spanned fifty-six years from beginning to end. He died of natural causes in his seventy-sixth year at Atella, a town of Campania. He was buried in Rome in the Campus Martius. He was a man who, for the most part, and not undeservedly, was considered to be similar to a god; for hardly anyone was more fortunate than him in war or more moderate in peace. In the forty-four years in which he alone held power, he was very affable, extremely generous to everyone, and most faithful to his friends, whom he elevated with such high honors that they almost equaled his lofty station.

9. At no time before him did the Roman state flourish more. With the exception of the civil wars, in which he was unconquered, he added to the Roman Empire: Egypt, Cantabria, Dalmatia (which had often been defeated but was completely subjugated at this time), Pannonia, Aquitania, Illyricum, Raetia, the Vindelici and Salassi in the Alps, and all the maritime cities of Pontus, the most noble of which were Bosporus and Panticapaeum. He defeated the Dacians in battle as well. He slaughtered large numbers of Germans and drove them beyond the river Elbe, which is in barbarian territory far beyond the Rhine. He conducted this war through his step-son Drusus and employed his other step-son, Tiberius, in the Pannonian war, in which he relocated forty thousand captives from Germany to Gaul above the bank of the Rhine. He recovered Armenia from the Parthians. The Persians gave him hostages, which they had given to no one before. The Persians also returned the Roman standards that they had taken from Crassus after they had defeated him.

10. The Scythians and Indians, to whom the name of the Romans was unknown before, sent gifts and ambassadors to him. Galatia was made a province under him as well, when earlier it had been a kingdom, and Marcus Lollius, as propraetor, was the first to govern it. Augustus was so highly regarded, even among the barbarians, that kings friendly to the Roman people founded cities in his honor, naming them "Caesarea," as was done by King Juba in Mauritania, and also in Palestine, which is now a very famous city. Moreover, many kings came from their kingdoms in order to submit to him, and in Roman dress, toga clad of course, they would run beside his wagon or horse. He was proclaimed divine while dying. He left a most prosperous state to his successor, Tiberius, who was first his step-son, then his son-in-law, and finally his son through adoption.

11. Tiberius managed the empire with great indolence, severe cruelty, wicked greed, and disgraceful lust. He himself never fought but managed wars through delegates. After summoning certain kings through flattery, he never allowed them to return home; among the number of whom was Archelaus, the Cappadocian, whose kingdom he reduced to a province. He ordered its greatest city, which is now called Caesarea but formerly was Mazaca, to be named after himself. To the great joy of everyone, he died in Campania in the twenty-third year of his reign, at the age of seventy-eight.

12. Caius Caesar, surnamed Caligula, the grandson of Augustus' stepson Drusus and of Tiberius himself, succeeded him. A most vile and murderous man, he eclipsed even the memory of Tiberius' crimes. He undertook a war against the Germans and then did little after entering Suebia. He committed incest with his sisters and even acknowledged a daughter born from one of them. While he was terrorizing everyone with extreme avarice, lust, and cruelty, he was slain in the palace at twenty-nine years of age, in the third year, tenth month, and eighth day of his reign.

13. After him followed Claudius, the paternal uncle of Caligula and the son of Drusus (who has a monument at Mogontiacum and who was also Caligula's grandfather). This man ruled unexceptionally, doing many things in a calm and self-controlled manner while acting cruelly and absurdly at other times. He invaded Britain, where no Roman had gone to after Caius Julius Caesar, and after conquering it through the efforts of Cnaeus Sentius and Aulus Plautius, illustrious and noble men, he celebrated a famous triumph. He also added certain islands, located in the ocean beyond Britain and called the Orcades, to the Roman Empire, and gave his son the name "Britannicus." Moreover, he acted so courteously around certain friends that he even accompanied the noble man Plautius, who had excellent accomplishments in the British expedition, during his triumph and walked on his left as he ascended the Capitol. He lived for sixty-four years and ruled for fourteen. After his death, he was consecrated and deified.

14. Nero, of similar character to his maternal uncle Caligula, succeeded Claudius and dishonored and diminished the Roman Empire. He lived in extraordinary luxury and extravagance, and following the example of Caius Caligula, he would bathe in hot and cold perfumes and fish with golden nets woven from purple strings. He had a large part of the Senate put to death and was an enemy to all good men. Until the end, he engaged in such disgraceful conduct that he would dance about and sing on stage in the dress of one who sings to the cithara or of a tragic actor. He murdered many of his relatives, putting to death his brother, wife, and mother. He burned the city of Rome in order that he might behold a similar spectacle to captured Troy burning long ago. He dared nothing in warfare and almost lost Britain, for two of its noblest towns were captured and demolished under him. The Parthians took Armenia and sent the Roman legions there under the yoke. Nevertheless, two provinces were formed under him: Pontus Polemoniacus, after King Polemon conceded it to him, and the Cottian Alps, upon the death of King Cottius.

15. Through these acts, he became utterly detested by the Roman world. He was abandoned by everyone simultaneously and declared an enemy by the Senate. When he was sought for punishment (which was that he would be beaten to death by rods while being dragged naked through the streets with a fork shaped prop placed under his head and thrown headfirst off of the Tarpeian rock), he fled from the palace to the suburban villa of one of his freedmen, located between the Via Salaria and Via Nomentana at the fourth milestone from the city, and took his own life. He built the baths in Rome that were formerly called the Neronian but are now the Alexandrian. He died at thirty-two years of age, in the fourteenth year of his reign, and with him, the family of Augustus died out.

16. Servius Galba, a senator from an ancient noble family, succeeded him at seventy-three years of age. He was chosen emperor by the Spaniards and Gauls, and soon after, was accepted by the entire army, for his private life was distinguished by military and civil accomplishments. He was often consul, and proconsul, and frequently a general in major wars. His reign was brief and had a good beginning, except that he seemed too prone towards severity. He was slain by the treachery of Otho in the seventh month of his reign, in the forum in Rome, and was buried in his gardens along the Via Aurelia, not far from the city of Rome.

17. After Galba was murdered, Otho seized power. The maternal side of his family was nobler than the paternal, however, neither was obscure. He was of mild disposition in private life and close to Nero. No example of his reign can be shown, for around the same time Otho killed Galba, Vitellius was selected emperor by the armies in Germany. After undertaking a war against him, Otho lost a minor battle near Betriacum in Italy, and although he still had powerful forces for war, he committed suicide. When his soldiers pleaded that he not despair so quickly concerning the outcome of the war, he stated that he himself was not so important that a civil war should be started over him. He took his own life at thirty-eight years of age, in the ninety-fifth day of his reign.

18. Vitellius took over the government next. He was from a family more honored than noble, for his father was not of very distinguished birth but had nevertheless served three regular consulships. He ruled quite disgracefully. He was known for great savagery, and especially, gluttony and voraciousness, as he is reported to have often feasted four or five times a day. Indeed, the memory of a famous dinner that his brother served for him has been passed down, where in addition to other delicacies, two thousand fish and seven thousand birds were reported to have been served. When he began attempting to emulate Nero, and thus did it so openly that he even honored Nero's humbly interred remains, he was slain by the generals of Vespasian, whose brother, Sabinus, Vitellius had previously killed in the city and burned with the Capitol. Vitellius was slain in utter disgrace. He was dragged nude in public through the streets with his head raised by the hair and a sword placed under his chin, then pelted with dung in the face and chest by everyone along the way, and finally, his throat was cut and he was thrown into the Tiber, lacking even a common burial. He died at the age of fifty-seven, on the eighth month and first day of his reign.

19. Vespasian succeeded him after being declared emperor in Palestine. He was a leader of obscure birth, but one that is to be compared with the best. He was illustrious in private life, having been sent by Claudius into Germany and then Britain, fighting thirty-two times with the enemy and adding two powerful nations, twenty towns, and the Isle of Wight, off the coast of Britain, to the Roman Empire. He ruled at Rome with great temperance. Only of money was he a bit too eager, which he took from no one unjustly and which he collected with foresight and diligence. Moreover, he gave most eagerly, especially to the indigent. It is not easy to find another chief before him whose generosity was greater or more just. He was so lenient that even those who plotted against him were rarely punished beyond the punishment of exile. Under him, Judea and Jerusalem, the noblest city of Palestine, were added to the Roman Empire. He reduced to the status of a province Achaia, Lycia, Rhodes, Byzantium, and Samos, all of which had been free before this time, and likewise, Thrace, Cilicia, and Commagene, which had been governed under friendly kings.

20. He was forgetful of affronts and enmities. He bore lightly invectives hurled against him by lawyers and philosophers, however, he was a diligent enforcer of military discipline. He celebrated a triumph with his son Titus over Jerusalem. When, because of these actions, he became beloved and delightful to the Senate, people, and eventually everyone, he died of diarrhea at his villa in the Sabine country, at sixty-nine years of age, in the ninth year and seventh day of his reign, and was enrolled among the gods. He had so much faith in the horoscope of his sons that, although many conspiracies were made against him, which he showed his contempt for by ignoring, he said in the Senate that either his sons would succeed him or nobody would.

21. His son Titus, who was also called Vespasian, succeeded him. He was a man so admirable in every type of virtue that he was said to be the darling and delight of the human race. He was highly eloquent, fond of war, and self-controlled. He pleaded cases in Latin and composed poems and tragedies in Greek. In the assault on Jerusalem, serving under his father, he pierced twelve defenders of the city with the blows of twelve arrows. He ruled at Rome with such great civility that he punished no one at all and released those convicted of conspiracies against him while retaining the same level of friendship with them as before. He was so affable and generous that he would not refuse anything to anyone, and when he was reproached for this by his friends, he replied that nobody should leave the emperor disappointed. It has been recorded as well that once, when he had not offered anything to anyone on a certain day, he said at dinner, "My friends, I have wasted this day." He built an amphitheater [the Colosseum] in Rome and had five thousand wild beasts killed in its dedication.

22. Esteemed to an extraordinary degree for these reasons, he died from sickness at forty-two years of age, in the same villa as his father, two years, eight months, and twenty days after he had been made emperor. There was such great public sorrow that everyone grieved as if he was their own. Upon the announcement of his passing around evening, the Senate rushed into the house of the Senate that night and heaped upon him even greater praise and regards than it had given him while he was alive and with them. He was enrolled among the gods.

23. Soon, his younger brother Domitian took over the empire. He was more similar to Nero, Caligula, or Tiberius than to his father or brother. In the early years of his reign, however, he was moderate. Soon though, he degenerated to great excesses of lust, anger, cruelty, and greed. He incited so much hatred against himself that he made people forget the honorable service of his father and brother. He had the most noble of the Senate put to death. He was the first to demand that he be called Lord and God. He allowed no statues of himself to be placed on the Capitol unless they were of gold or silver. He had his own cousins killed. He was disgustingly arrogant. He made four expeditions; one against the Sarmatians, another against the Chatti, and two against the Dacians. He celebrated a double triumph on account of the Dacians and Chatti and assumed only the laurel for the Sarmatians. He suffered many calamities in these wars as well; for one of his legions was annihilated with its general in Sarmatia, and Oppius Sabinus, a man of consular rank, and Cornelius Fuscus, the praetorian prefect, were slain with large armies by the Dacians. He undertook many works in Rome. Among these were the Capitol, the Forum Transitorium, the Portico of the Gods, the temple of Isis and Serapis, and the Stadium. When he had become detested by all on account of his offenses, he was slain by a conspiracy of those close to him at forty-five years of age, in the fifteenth year of his reign. His corpse was carried out in total disgrace by the corpse bearers of the poor and was ignobly buried.

Book VIII

1. In the eight hundred and fiftieth year after the founding of the city, during the consulship of Vetus and Valens, the Roman state returned to a most prosperous state after fortuitously being entrusted to good chiefs; for Nerva, a man of moderate nobility who was self-disciplined and energetic in private life, succeeded the destructive tyrant Domitian. He was made emperor as a very old man through the efforts of Petronius Secundus, the praetorian prefect, and Parthenius, Domitian's assassin. Nerva conducted himself very fairly and civilly. He looked after the state with divine foresight by adopting Trajan. He died in Rome one year, four months, and eight days into his reign, at the age of seventy-two, and was enrolled among the gods.

2. Ulpius Crinitus Trajan succeeded him. He was born at Italica in Spain, from a family more ancient than renowned, for his father was the first consul from it. He was made emperor near Agrippina in Gaul. He managed the state in such a manner that he is deservedly ranked above all other emperors. He was unusually courteous and brave. He expanded far and wide the Roman Empire's borders, which after the time of Augustus, had been defended rather than honorably enlarged. He rebuilt cities in Germany across the Rhine. After defeating Decebalus, he subjugated Dacia and made a province in those lands across the Danube that the Taifali, Victohali, and Tervingi now possess. That province extended one thousand miles in circumference.

3. He recovered Armenia, which the Parthians had seized, killing

Parthamasires, who was in control of it. He appointed a king to the Albani. He received in allegiance the kings of the Iberi, Sarmatians, Bosporans, Arabians, Osdroeni, and Colchians. He seized the lands of the Cardueni and Marcomedi, as well as Anthemusium — a celebrated region of Persia, and the cities of Seleucia, Ctesiphon, and Babylon. He defeated and subjugated the Messenii. He advanced all the way to the borders of India and the Red Sea, where he made three provinces — Armenia, Assyria, and Mesopotamia, including those tribes that border Madena. Afterwards, he reduced Arabia to the status of a province. He built a fleet on the Red Sea for the purpose of laying waste the lands of India.

4. However, his civility and self-control surpassed his military glory. He treated everyone as an equal, in Rome and throughout the provinces, often visiting friends who were sick or celebrating feast days, giving banquets for them in return regardless of rank, and accompanying them in their carriages. He harassed none of the senators and did nothing unjust to increase the treasury. He was kind to everyone, and both publicly and privately enriched and increased the honors of those of even moderate acquaintance. He constructed many buildings throughout the world, granted immunities to states, and did nothing hasty or rash. During his time, only one senator was condemned, but this was done by the Senate without his knowledge. For these reasons, he became like a god throughout the world and earned nothing but veneration both in life and in death.

5. Among his other sayings, this admirable one has been reported: when his friends were reproaching him for acting in too common a manner, he replied that he was the type of emperor to his citizens that he himself had hoped to have when he was a private citizen. After attaining great glory both at war and at home, he died from diarrhea near Seleucia in Isauria. He passed away in the sixty-third year, ninth month, and fourth day of his life, in the nineteenth year, sixth month, and fifteenth day of his reign. He was enrolled among the gods. He was the only one of all the emperors to be buried in the city. His bones were placed in a golden urn under his column, which was one hundred forty-four feet in height, in the forum that he had built. Such respect has been paid to his memory that, even up to our own time, emperors are not otherwise acclaimed in the Senate than "more fortunate than Augustus, better than Trajan!" So much has the fame of his goodness endured that he furnishes the most splendid example to those wishing to flatter or those truly offering praise.

6. After the death of Trajan, Aelius Hadrian was chosen emperor, not by any wish of Trajan, but through the efforts of Plotina, Trajan's wife. Hadrian was also born in Italica in Spain. Trajan, while still alive, was unwilling to adopt him even though Hadrian was the son of his cousin. Envying the glory of Trajan, Hadrian immediately relinquished three provinces that Trajan had added to the empire, recalled the armies from Assyria, Mesopotamia, and Armenia, and decided upon the Euphrates as the border of the empire. After trying to do the same thing in Dacia, he was deterred by his friends, lest many Roman citizens would be handed over to the barbarians. Trajan, after conquering Dacia, had brought a vast multitude of men there from the entire Roman world to cultivate the fields and populate the cities because Dacia was depleted of men by the long war with Decebalus.

7. He enjoyed peace throughout his entire reign and fought only once, through one of his governors. He traveled around the Roman world and built many things. He was most eloquent in Latin speech and learned in Greek. He did not have a great reputation for clemency, but was very diligent concerning the treasury and military discipline. He died in Campania at more than sixty years of age, in the twenty-first year, tenth month, and twenty-ninth day of his reign. The Senate was unwilling to grant him divine honors, but his successor, Titus Aurelius Antoninus Fulvius, vehemently demanded that this be done, and although all of the senators were in open opposition, he at last obtained his demand.

8. Therefore, Titus Antoninus Fulvius Boionius [Antoninus Pius], also named Pius, succeeded Hadrian. He was from a famous, but not very ancient family. He was a distinguished man who deservedly may be compared to Numa Pompilius, just as Trajan may be compared to Romulus. He lived in great honor as a private citizen and greater still during his reign. He was harsh to no one and kind to all. He had moderate glory in warfare, having desired to defend the provinces rather than enlarge them. He sought fair men to manage the state, honored good men, and detested wicked men, although he harmed none of them. He was venerated no less than feared by friendly kings, so much so that many barbarian nations would put aside their weapons and bring their quarrels and disputes before him and abide by his judgment. He was very rich before his reign, but greatly diminished his wealth by paying the soldiers and giving generously to his friends. He left the treasury quite rich however. He was called Pius on account of his clemency. He died at Lorium, his villa, by the twelfth milestone from the city, at seventy-three years of age, in the twenty-third year of his reign. He was enrolled among the gods and justly consecrated.

9. Marcus Antoninus Verus [Marcus Aurelius] reigned after him. He was of unquestionably noble birth indeed, since the paternal side of his family descended from Numa Pompilius and the maternal side from a Salentine king. With him ruled Lucius Annius Antoninus Verus [Lucius Verus]. Then, for the first time, the Roman state had two rulers with equal authority. Up until this time it had always had a single Augustus.

10. These men were joined by family and affinity; for Lucius Verus had married the daughter of Marcus Aurelius, and Marcus Aurelius was the son-in-law of Antoninus Pius, having married his own cousin, Faustina Galeria the Younger, the daughter of Antoninus Pius. They waged war against the Parthians, who were rebelling for the first time since Trajan's victory over them. Lucius Verus set out to manage that war. While he was at Antioch and around Armenia, he accomplished many great things through his generals. He captured Seleucia, the most noble city of Assyria, with four hundred thousand men. He secured a triumph for Parthia and celebrated it with his [adopted] brother, who was also his father-in-law. He died in Venetia after departing from the city of Concordia for Altinum. While he was sitting with his brother in his carriage, he had a sudden stroke, an affliction the Greeks call "apoplexy." He was a man of insufficient self control, however, he did nothing outrageous due to respect for his brother. When he died in the eleventh year of his reign, he was enrolled among the gods.

11. Marcus Aurelius managed the state alone after him. He was a man who can more easily be admired than praised. He was of a most tranquil disposition from the beginning of his life, so much so that from infancy he changed his countenance neither in joy nor sorrow. He was devoted to the Stoic philosophy. He was a philosopher, not only in his manner of life, but in his education as well. He was so admired while still a youth that Hadrian had prepared to make him his successor, but after adopting Antoninus Pius, he wished him to become Antoninus' son-in-law in order for him to become emperor in that way.

12. He was instructed in philosophy by Apollonius of Chalcedon, and in Greek literature by Sextus of Chaeronea, the grandson of Plutarch. Fronto, the highly renowned orator, taught him Latin literature. He acted as an equal to everyone in Rome, not becoming arrogant by his lofty position, and was manifestly generous. He managed the provinces with great kindness and restraint. Affairs were successfully conducted against the Germans under his leadership. He himself waged one war, against the Marcomanni, but it was more serious than any other war in memory and may be compared to the Punic wars. This war became all the more serious as entire armies were lost during it; for in his reign, after the victory over Persia, there was such a severe outbreak of plague that a majority of the people and almost all of the soldiers in Rome and throughout Italy and the provinces wasted away from weakness.

13. Therefore, when he had persevered with great effort and patience for three years at Carnuntum, he finished the Marcomannic war, which the Quadi, Vandals, Sarmatians, Suebi, and all the other barbarians of that area waged with the Marcomanni. He killed many thousands of men, and after liberating Pannonia from servitude, he triumphed again in Rome with his son, Commodus Antoninus, whom he had already made Caesar. Since he had no money to disburse because the treasury was exhausted due to the cost of the war, and since he was unwilling to levy a tax on the provinces or Senate, he auctioned off golden vases, crystal and murra cups, his and his wife's golden and silk clothing, and many jeweled ornaments from the imperial household in the Forum of Divine Trajan. This sale was held for two continuous months and brought in much gold. After his victory, however, he returned the money to the buyers who wished to return what they had bought, while causing no trouble to those who preferred to retain their purchases.

14. He permitted the more distinguished men to serve banquets with the same level of luxury and number of servants as he himself had. He was so splendid in putting on public shows after his victory that he is reported to have exhibited one hundred lions at the same time. After he had restored the state back to prosperity through his valor and clemency, he died in the eighteenth year of his reign, in the sixty-first year of his life, and was enrolled among the gods with all eagerly assenting.

15. His successor, Lucius Antoninus Commodus, was nothing like his father except that he also fought successfully against the Germans. He tried to change the name of the month of September so that it would be called "Commodus" after himself. He was depraved in his extravagance and lewdness. He often fought at a gladiator school with gladiatorial weapons and later also fought in the amphitheater with men of the same type. When he had reigned for twelve years and eight months after his father, he died so suddenly that it was thought that he was either strangled or killed by poison. He was so detested by everyone that, after he was dead, he was declared an enemy of the human race.

16. Pertinax, an elderly man who had reached seventy years of age, was appointed to rule the empire by a decree of the Senate when he was serving as urban prefect. He was slain on the eightieth day of his reign in an insurrection of the Praetorian Guard and by the treachery of Julianus.

17. Salvius Julianus, a nobleman who was most skilled at law, seized the government after him. He was the grandson of Salvius Julianus who composed the perpetual edict under Divine Hadrian. He was defeated by Severus at the Milvian bridge and was slain in the palace. He lived for seven months after he had begun to rule.

18. Henceforth, Septimius Severus took over the management of the Roman Empire. He was born in Africa, in the province of Tripolis, in the town of Leptis. He was the only emperor in all of history, both before and after, who was from Africa. He was first an official of the treasury, next a military tribune, and then, after many offices and positions, he ascended all the way to the management of the whole state. He wished for himself to be called "Pertinax," in honor of that Pertinax who was killed by Julianus. He was very frugal and fierce by nature. He waged many wars successfully. Near Cyzicus, he killed Pescennius Niger, who had rebelled in Egypt and Syria. He defeated the Parthians, the interior Arabians, and the Adiabeni. He defeated the Arabians so thoroughly that he even established a province there. On account of these things, he was called "Parthicus," "Arabicus," and "Adiabenicus." He restored many buildings throughout the entire Roman world. Also during his reign, Clodius Albinus, who had been an accomplice of Julianus in the murder of Pertinax, made himself Caesar in Gaul. He was defeated near Lugdunum and was slain.

19. In addition to glory in war, Severus was distinguished in civil pursuits as well. He was educated in literature and had achieved a full knowledge of philosophy. His last war was in Britain. In order to fortify the provinces that he had taken there with the utmost security, he constructed a wall from sea to sea, a distance of one hundred and thirty-three miles. He died quite old at Eboracum, in the sixteenth year and third month of his reign, and was pronounced divine. He left his sons, Geta and Bassianus, as his successors, but requested that the Senate bestow the name of "Antoninus" on Bassianus. Thus, he was called Marcus Aurelius Antoninus Bassianus and succeeded his father. Geta was declared a public enemy and died shortly thereafter.

20. Marcus Aurelius Antoninus Bassianus, also called "Caracalla," was similar in character to his father, although a bit more harsh and threatening. He constructed magnificent baths in Rome which are called the "Antonine Baths," but did nothing else memorable. He was unable to control his lust and took his own stepmother, Julia, as a wife. He died near Edessa in Osdroena as he was undertaking an expedition against the Parthians, in the sixth year and second month of his reign, having just passed his forty-third year. He was given a public funeral.

21. Next, Opilius Macrinus, the praetorian prefect, was made emperor with his son, Diadumenus. They accomplished nothing memorable due to the brevity of their reign, for it lasted only one year and two months. They were both slain together in a military revolt.

22. Marcus Aurelius Antoninus [Elagabalus] was selected emperor after them. He was thought to be the son of Antoninus Caracalla and was a priest of the temple of Heliogabalus. Although he arrived in Rome to the great expectation of the soldiers and Senate, he polluted himself by every type of disgraceful deed. He lived most shamelessly and obscenely, and two years and eight months into his reign, was killed with his mother, Symiasera, in a military revolt.

23. Aurelius Alexander [Severus Alexander] succeeded him while still very young, having been named Caesar by the army and Augustus by the Senate. After undertaking a war against the Persians, he gloriously defeated Xerxes, their king. He enforced very severe military discipline. He disbanded several entire legions that had raised a tumult. He had as an assistant or secretary, Ulpian, the compiler of law. He was quite popular in Rome. He died in a military revolt in Gaul, in the thirteenth year and ninth day of his reign. He was singularly devoted to his mother, Mamaea.

Book IX

1. After him was Maximinus, the first to take power from the ranks of the soldiers backed by them alone, without the approval of the Senate or having been a senator. Although he had been named emperor by the army, after successfully waging war against the Germans, he was deserted by his soldiers and slain by Pupienus at Aquileia with his son who was still a boy and with whom he had reigned for three years and a few days.

2. Afterwards, there were three Augusti at the same time: Pupienus, Balbinus, and Gordian. The former two were from obscure families, the latter was from a noble one. In fact, his father, the elder Gordian, had been chosen emperor by the consensus of the soldiers while serving as proconsul of Africa during the reign of Maximinus. When Balbinus and Pupienus came to Rome, they were slain in the palace, and the empire was given to Gordian alone. Gordian, although still a boy, married Tranquillina in Rome. Then, after opening the doors of the temple of Janus [a sign that Rome was at war], he departed for the East in order to wage war against the Parthians, who were threatening an irruption into the empire. He conducted the war successfully indeed, thrashing the Persians in several great battles. On his way home he was slain, not far from Roman territory, through the treachery of Philip who succeeded him. The soldiers built a mound for him, which is now a Roman fort overlooking the Euphrates, at the twentieth milestone from Circesium. His remains were carried back to Rome, and he was proclaimed divine.

3. The two Philips, father and son, seized the empire after Gordian was slain. After the army was led back safely, they departed from Syria to Italy. During their reign, the one thousandth anniversary of the city of Rome was celebrated with a great display of games and spectacles. Afterwards, they were both slain (the elder in Verona and the younger in Rome) by the army. They ruled only five years but were enrolled among the gods.

4. Decius, from Lesser Pannonia, born in Budalia, assumed power after them. He suppressed a civil war that had flared up in Gaul. He made his son Caesar and built a bath in Rome. When he and his son had ruled for two years, they were both killed in barbarian country. They were enrolled among the gods.

5. Gallus Hostilian and Volusian, the son of Gallus, were soon chosen as emperors. Aemilianus revolted in Moesia during their reign. After they both set out to suppress him, they were slain at Interamna, having not even ruled for two years. They accomplished nothing significant. Their reign is remembered only for plague, disease, and sickness.

6. Aemilianus was of very obscure birth and ruled even more obscurely. He died in the third month of his reign.

7. Next, Licinius Valerian was made emperor by the army, and soon afterwards, Augustus, while operating in Raetia and Noricum. Gallienus was named Caesar by the Senate in Rome as well. As a result of either their ill-fortune or inactivity, their reign was ruinous and almost brought about the end of the Roman state. The Germans advanced all the way to Ravenna. Valerian, while waging war in Mesopotamia, was defeated by Shapur, king of the Persians. He was soon captured and grew old in ignoble servitude among the Parthians.

8. Gallienus was made Augustus though still a young man. He managed the empire well at first, then adequately, and finally disastrously. He did many things with vigor as a young man in Gaul and Illyricum, slaying Ingenuus (who had assumed the imperial purple) near Mursa, and Trebellianus [Regalianus]. He was gentle and peaceful for a long time but then descended into every type of licentiousness. He neglected the management of the government through disgraceful inactivity and despair. After devastating Gaul, the Alamanni penetrated into Italy. Dacia, beyond the Danube, which Trajan had added to the empire, was lost at this time. Greece, Macedonia, Pontus, and Asia were laid waste by the Goths; Pannonia by the Sarmatians and Quadi. The Germans advanced all the way to Spain and stormed the noble city of Tarraco. The Parthians, after seizing Mesopotamia, began to claim Syria.

9. Then, with the situation desperate and the Roman Empire almost destroyed, Postumus, born in Gaul from a very obscure family, assumed the imperial purple. He ruled for ten years in such a way that he restored almost all of the provinces that had been lost through his valor and leadership. He was slain in a sedition of the soldiers because he refused to hand over Mogontiacum, which had rebelled against him at the instigation of Laelianus, to the soldiers to be plundered. Marius, a lowly craftsman, assumed the imperial purple after him and was slain two days later. After that, Victorinus took control of Gaul. He was a very energetic man, but since he was too lustful and corrupted other men's wives, he was slain at Agrippina, through the machinations of one of his secretaries, in the second year of his reign.

10. Tetricus, a senator, succeeded him. While managing Aquitania in the capacity of governor, he was chosen emperor in absentia by the soldiers and assumed the imperial purple near Burdigala. He endured many revolts of the troops. While these events were taking place in Gaul, the Persians were defeated by Odenathus in the East. Odenathus advanced all the way to Ctesiphon after securing Syria and recovering Mesopotamia.

11. Thus, while Gallienus was forsaking the state, the Roman Empire was saved in the West by Postumus and in the East by Odenathus. Gallienus was slain in Mediolanum with his brother in the ninth year of his reign, and Claudius [II Gothicus] succeeded him. He was chosen by the soldiers and proclaimed Augustus by the Senate. He defeated the Goths, who were laying waste Illyricum and Macedonia, in a great battle. He was a frugal and moderate man, a staunch advocate of justice and suitable for managing the empire. Nevertheless, he died from disease two years into his reign and was proclaimed divine. The Senate bestowed a great honor on him indeed, placing his golden shield in the senate house and a golden statue of him in the Capitol.

12. After him, Quintillus, the brother of Claudius, was elected emperor by the will of the soldiers. He was a man of unique self-control and courteousness, who was considered to be the equal of, or even more preferable than, his brother. He was proclaimed Augustus with the consent of the Senate and was killed on the seventeenth day of his reign.

13. Aurelian assumed power after him. Born in Dacia Ripensis, he was a man skilled in warfare, but overly spirited and prone to cruelty. He too valiantly defeated the Goths. He restored Roman power to its former boundaries through various successes in war. He defeated Tetricus near Catalauni, with Tetricus himself betraying his own army, whose continuous mutinies he could no longer endure. Indeed, Tetricus even begged Aurelian to intervene on his behalf through secret letters and employed this verse, among others, from Virgil: "Rescue me, Invincible One, from these evils!" Not far from Antioch, and without much of a fight, Aurelian captured Zenobia, who held the East after her husband Odenathus had been slain. He entered Rome and celebrated a noble triumph as the restorer of the East and West with Tetricus and Zenobia preceding his chariot. Afterwards, Tetricus was governor of Lucania and lived a long life as a private citizen. Zenobia left descendants in Rome who are still there today.

14. Also during his reign, the workers of the mint revolted in the city, killing the finance minister, Felicissimus, and corrupting the money. Aurelian suppressed their revolt with great cruelty. He condemned many nobles to death. He was savage, bloodthirsty, and more of a necessary emperor in certain respects than a beloved one in any. He was always ferocious and even killed his sister's son. To a great extent, he was a reformer of military discipline and dissolute morals.

15. He enclosed the city with stronger walls. He built a temple dedicated to the Sun, in which he placed a vast amount of gold and jewels. He let slip away the province of Dacia, which Trajan had established beyond the Danube, because Illyricum and Moesia had been laid waste, and he despaired over being able to hold it. He moved the Roman citizens from the cities and fields of Dacia and relocated them in the middle of Moesia. He called this "Dacia," the area which now divides the two Moesias on the right bank of the Danube as it flows to the sea, when before, Dacia was on the left bank. He was slain through the treachery of one of his servants, who brought to certain military men (friends of Aurelian) a list of names forged in Aurelian's handwriting, as though Aurelian was preparing to kill them. Thus, in order for this to be prevented, he was slain in the middle of the old paved road which extends between Constantinople and Heraclea, in a place called Caenophrurium. His death did not go unavenged, and he gained enrollment among the gods.

16. Tacitus took over the empire after him. He was a man of excellent manners and one who was suitable to govern the state. However, he left no famous deeds to posterity because he died after ruling less than six months. Florianus, who succeeded him, ruled for two months and twenty days and did nothing worthy of memory.

17. After him, Probus, a man of great military glory, undertook the management of the state. He recovered Gaul, which had been seized by the barbarians, through great successes in the field. He crushed in battle certain men who were trying to usurp power, namely, Saturninus in the East, and Proculus and Bonosus at Agrippina. He permitted the Gauls and Pannonians to have vineyards and had his soldiers plant vineyards on Mt. Alma in Sirmium and Mt. Aureus in Upper Moesia; he gave these to the inhabitants of the provinces to cultivate. After he had fought innumerable wars and procured peace, he stated that soldiers would soon be unnecessary. He was a spirited man, energetic and just, and one who equaled Aurelian in military glory but surpassed him in civility of manners. Nevertheless, he was killed during a military uprising in an iron tower at Sirmium.

18. Carus, born in Narbo in Gaul, was made Augustus after him. He immediately made his sons, Carinus and Numerian, Caesars. While he was waging war against the Sarmatians, a revolt of the Persians was reported. He departed for the East and had notable accomplishments against the Persians. He routed them in battle and captured their noblest cities, Coche and Ctesiphon. He was struck down by the blow of a divine thunderbolt after making a camp above the Tigris river. His son Numerian, a young man of excellent character whom he had brought with him as Caesar to Persia, was also slain, treacherously, at the instigation of Aper, his father-in-law, as he was being carried on a litter due to a malady of the eyes. Although his death was being concealed by guile until which time Aper could seize power, it was revealed by the stench of his corpse; for the soldiers who were accompanying him were disturbed by a foul odor, and upon opening the curtains of his litter, they learned of his death several days after it had taken place.

19. In the meantime, Carinus, whom Carus had left behind as Caesar with authority over Illyricum, Gaul, and Italy as he was setting out against the Parthians, disgraced himself with every type of wickedness. He killed many innocent people on fictitious charges, corrupted noble marriages, and additionally, ruined former schoolmates who had annoyed him in the classroom or bothered him even slightly. He became hated by all men because of these things, and not much later, he paid the price; for as the victorious army was returning from Persia, since it had lost Carus, the Augustus, to a thunderbolt, and Numerian, the Caesar, to treachery, it chose as emperor Diocletian, a man from Dalmatia of such obscure birth that he was believed by most to be the son of a clerk and by some to be the son of a freedman of the senator Anullinus.

20. Diocletian, in the first assembly of the soldiers, swore he had nothing to do with the death of Numerian, and since Aper, who had formed the plot against Numerian, was standing beside him, he was slain in view of the army with a sword by the hand of Diocletian. Afterwards, Diocletian defeated Carinus, who was hated and detested by all, in a great battle near Margum. Carinus was betrayed by his own army, although he had the stronger one, which completely deserted him between Viminacium and Mt. Aureus. Thus, Diocletian gained control of the Roman state. When the peasants in Gaul stirred up a revolt, calling their faction "Bacaudae" and led by Amandus and Aelianus, he sent Maximianus Herculius as Caesar to subjugate them. He subdued the country folk in some minor engagements and restored the peace in Gaul.

21. Also during this time, Carausius, a man of very humble origin who had achieved an excellent reputation through a career of active military service, was appointed while at Bononia to pacify the seas off the coast of Belgica and Armorica, which were infested by the Franks and Saxons. He often captured many barbarians but did not send back all of the plunder to the people of the province or the emperors. When the suspicion arose that he secretly admitted the barbarians in order to enrich himself by capturing them with their booty, he was condemned to death by Maximianus. Carausias then took up the imperial purple and seized Britain.

22. Since the entire world was in turmoil (Carausius was rebelling in Britain, Achilleus in Egypt, the Quinquegentiani were ravaging Africa, and Narses was waging war against the East), Diocletian promoted Maximianus Herculius from Caesar to Augustus and made Constantius and Maximianus Galerius Caesars. Constantius is purported to be the grandson of Claudius II Gothicus through his daughter. Maximianus Galerius was born in Dacia, not far from Serdica. In order for them to be joined by marriage as well, Constantius married the step-daughter of Herculius, Theodora, from whom he had six children who were the brothers of Constantine, and Galerius married Valeria, the daughter of Diocletian. Both were compelled to repudiate the wives they had earlier. After attempting several wars in vain against Carausius, a man most skilled in the art of war, peace was finally agreed upon. Allectus, an associate of Carausius, killed him after seven years and then held Britain himself for three years. He was overthrown by Asclepiodotus, the praetorian prefect. Thus, Britain was recovered in the tenth year.

23. At the same time, Constantius Caesar fought successfully in Gaul. At Lingonae, he experienced both favorable and adverse fortune in the same day; for when the barbarians suddenly fell upon him, he was forced by such dire necessity into the city that the gates were already closed, and he had to be raised onto the wall by ropes; and scarcely five hours later, when the army arrived, he killed about sixty thousand of the Alamanni. Maximianus Augustus ended the war in Africa after conquering the Quinquegentiani and forcing them to make peace. Diocletian defeated Achilleus, having besieged him for about eight months in Alexandria, and killed him. He followed up his victory harshly, brutalizing all Egypt with severe proscriptions and massacres. At this time, however, he prudently ordained and established many new laws which remain until our own time.

24. After meeting Narses between Callinicum and Carrhae, Galerius Maximianus fought an unsuccessful first battle against him, contending rashly rather than without spirit, having joined battle with a small body of men against a vast enemy. Therefore, upon being beaten and heading back to Diocletian, Galerius is said to have been received with such disdain by Diocletian that when Galerius met him on the march, he was reported to have run for several miles clad in purple alongside Diocletian's chariot.

25. Soon, however, after gathering troops throughout Illyricum and Moesia, he fought a second time against Narses, the grandfather of Hormizd and Shapur, in Greater Armenia with great success and with no less prudence and valor, for he even undertook the duty of a scout with one or two other horsemen. He plundered Narses' camp after routing him. He captured his wives, sisters, and children, as well as a vast number of the Persian nobility and an immense amount of Persian treasure. He compelled Narses himself to flee to the remotest wildernesses of his kingdom; on which account, when he returned in triumph to Diocletian, who was among the garrisons in Mesopotamia, he was received with great honor. Afterwards, they waged various wars, together and individually, subjugating the Carpi and Bastarnae and defeating the Sarmatians. They relocated vast numbers of these peoples into Roman territory.

26. Diocletian was crafty in manner, shrewd, and discriminating. He was content to satisfy his own cruel nature with the hatred of others.

He was, however, a most diligent and skillful leader. He was the first to introduce regal custom into the Roman Empire, rather than the usual practice of Roman liberty, and ordered that he should be revered, when previously all emperors were only saluted. He adorned his clothing and shoes with jeweled ornaments. Previously, the only sign of imperial power was the purple cloak and one's other garments were ordinary.

27. Herculius, on the other hand, was openly savage and uncivilized in nature, even displaying his fierceness in his frightful countenance. Indulging in his nature, he would accompany Diocletian in all of his more savage endeavors. When Diocletian was getting on in age and had begun to think that he was no longer suitable to govern the empire, he proposed to Herculius that they should return to private life and hand over the management of the empire to more vigorous and younger men. To which notion, his colleague grudgingly complied. Therefore, they exchanged their imperial trappings for the garb of private citizens on the same day (Diocletian in Nicomedia and Herculius in Mediolanum), after their famous triumph, which they celebrated in Rome over numerous nations with an illustrious procession of paintings [representations of cities, rivers, and other things in conquered countries], and in which the wives, sisters, and children of Narses were led before their chariots. Then they both retired, one to Salonae and the other to Lucania.

28. Diocletian grew old in his villa, not very far from Salonae, as a private citizen in a famous retirement, having exercised extraordinary virtue as, he alone, since the founding of the Roman Empire, voluntarily stepped down from so high a station to the status and dignity of private life. Therefore, something happened to him which happened to no one else since the beginning of mankind, that, although he died a private citizen, he was nevertheless enrolled among the gods.

Book X

1. Therefore, as these men were retiring from the administration of the state, Constantius and Galerius were chosen as Augusti, and the Roman world was divided between them in such a way that Constantius received Gaul, Italy, and Africa, and Galerius received Illyricum, Asia, and the East; two Caesars were also selected. Constantius, however, content with the dignity of Augustus, refused the burden of managing Italy and Africa. He was a distinguished and very courteous man who favored the people of the provinces and private citizens keeping their wealth, and who did very little to benefit the treasury, saying that it was better for the public wealth to be held in private hands than to be confined in one place. Moreover, he lived in such a modest manner that if he had to serve a feast for a greater number of friends than usual on holidays, his dining hall would be furnished with silverware that had been sought out door to door from private citizens. He was not only beloved but venerated by the Gauls because, while he was governor, they avoided the suspicious prudence of Diocletian and the bloody rashness of Maximianus. He died at Eboracum in Britain in the thirteenth year of his reign and was enrolled among the gods.

2. Galerius was a man both well-mannered and highly skilled in the art of war. When he learned that he was also to receive the administration of Italy with the permission of Constantius, he chose two Caesars: Maximinus, whom he appointed to the East, and Severus, to whom he gave Italy. He himself remained in Illyricum; but when Constantius died, Constantine, his son from a previous marriage to a woman of obscure birth, was chosen emperor in Britain and became a very desirable ruler in place of his father. In Rome meanwhile, the Praetorian Guard, having revolted, pronounced as Augustus, Maxentius, the son of Herculius, who was staying at the Villa Publica not far from the city. Once this was announced, Maximianus Herculius, excited by the prospect of regaining the position that he had reluctantly given up, hurried to Rome from Lucania — the retirement place that he had chosen as a private citizen where he was growing old in a most pleasant region. He urged Diocletian as well, through letters which Diocletian considered folly, to take back the power that he had relinquished. Against the revolt of the Praetorians and Maxentius, Severus Caesar was sent by Galerius and came to Rome with the army. As he was besieging the city, he was treacherously deserted by his soldiers. This increased the strength of Maxentius and confirmed his power. Severus was slain at Ravenna while fleeing.

3. After these events, Herculius Maximianus endured insurrection and abuse from the soldiers when he attempted to strip his son Maxentius of power in an assembly of the armies. From there he departed for Gaul, pretending that he had been expelled by his son in order that he might join up with his son-in-law Constantine, and plotting, if the opportunity presented itself, to kill him. Constantine was ruling in Gaul with the overwhelming approval of both the soldiers and the people of the province, having cut to pieces the Franks and Alamanni and having captured their kings, whom, when he put on a magnificent show of games, he threw to the wild beasts. Therefore, when the plot was exposed by Herculius' daughter Fausta, who revealed it to her husband Constantine, Herculius fled and was killed in Massalia, where he was preparing to set sail to his son. He met with a well-deserved ending, for he was a man inclined to every type of violence and savagery, and was treacherous, troublesome, and totally lacking in civility.

4. During this time, Licinius, born in Dacia, was made emperor by Galerius. He was known to Galerius by longtime acquaintance, and also as being energetic in work and reliable in duty during the war that Galerius waged against Narses. The death of Galerius followed immediately afterwards. Thus, at this time, the government was held by four new emperors: Constantine and Maxentius — the sons of Augusti, and Licinius and Maximinus — men new to high rank. However, Constantine, in the fifth year of his reign, started a civil war against Maxentius and beat his forces in many battles. Finally, he conquered Maxentius himself (who was terrorizing the nobility by every type of brutality) at the Milvian Bridge in Rome and gained control of Italy. Not much afterwards in the East, Maximinus, who was trying to overthrow Licinius, prevented his own impending destruction by an accidental death near Tarsus.

5. Constantine, a remarkable man who strove to accomplish all things that he set his mind to and who aspired to rule the entire world, made war against Licinius, although they had close ties and were related through marriage; for his sister Constantia had married Licinius. First, Constantine overwhelmed him by surprise near Cibalae in Pannonia Secunda, where Licinius was making great preparations for war. Then, having gained control of Dardania, Moesia, and Macedon, he seized numerous provinces.

6. They then fought various wars between them, and peace was made and broken. Finally, Licinius surrendered after being defeated in a land and sea battle near Nicomedia. He was slain as a private citizen in Thessalonica, in violation of a sacred oath. At this time, the Roman state was ruled by one Augustus and three Caesars, an occurrence which had never happened before, as the sons of Constantine were in control of Gaul, the East, and Italy. But due to the arrogance of success, Constantine changed from his former pleasant disposition. He first persecuted his own relatives, killing his own son, an excellent man, and the son of his sister, a good-natured youth, then soon his wife, and later, numerous friends.

7. He was a man comparable to the best emperors early in his reign, to mediocre ones towards the end. Innumerable talents of the mind and body were evident in him. He was very eager for military glory and enjoyed good fortune in war, but his good fortune did not surpass his diligence; for after the civil war, he defeated the Goths at various times, and upon granting them peace at last, he left the memory of great kindness among the barbarian tribes. He was devoted to peaceful arts and liberal studies, and eager to earn popularity, which he sought for himself from all by his generosity and docility. He was hesitant with some friends but excellent to the rest, not passing any opportunity to make them richer or more illustrious.

8. He proposed many laws, some of which were good and fair, some harsh, but most superfluous. He was the first to endeavor to elevate the status of a city named after himself to such a height that it rivaled Rome. While undertaking a war against the Parthians, who were then harassing Mesopotamia, he died, in the thirty-first year of his reign and the sixty-sixth year of his life, at the Villa Publica in Nicomedia. His death was announced by a hairy star, which the Greeks call a "comet," of extraordinary size which shined for a long time. He gained enrollment among the gods.

9. He left his three sons — Constantine, Constantius, and Constans, and the son of his brother, Dalmatius Caesar, as successors. However, Dalmatius Caesar, who was of excellent character and not at all unlike his uncle, was killed by a military faction. Constantius, his cousin, allowed this to happen but did not order it. Afterwards, Constantine, having started a war against his brother Constans and having attacked him rashly at Aquileia, was killed by the generals of Constans. Thus, the state returned to having two Augusti. The reign of Constans was energetic and just for a long time. Then, when his health became poor, and he came under the influence of wicked friends, he began to commit serious offenses. When he became intolerable to the people of the provinces and unpopular with the soldiers, he was slain by the faction of Magnentius. He died not far from Spain in a fort named Helena, in the sixteenth year of his reign and thirtieth year of his life, but not before accomplishing many things with vigor in military service. He was feared throughout his entire life by the army, although not for any great cruelty.

10. Constantius had a different fortune. He endured many great misfortunes at the hands of the Persians. Towns were often captured, cities besieged, and armies slaughtered. He won no battles against Shapur, although he lost an almost certain victory near Singara due to the headstrong spirit of the soldiers, who demanded seditiously, foolishly, and contrary to the custom of war, to enter battle as the day was ending. After the death of Constans, while Magnentius was in possession of Italy, Africa, and Gaul, Illyricum revolted, and Vetranio was elected to the throne by the consensus of the soldiers. They chose him as emperor to defend Illyricum when he was already an old man and beloved by all for the length and success of his military service. He was an honorable man of the old customs and delightful civility, but so uneducated in the liberal arts that he did not learn even the first rudiments of literature until he was old and already emperor.

11. Vetranio's power was taken from him by Constantius, who started a civil war to avenge the death of his brother. In a new and unusual way, Vetranio was compelled to put aside the imperial insignia by the will of the soldiers. There was also an uprising in Rome at this time. Nepotian, the son of Constantine's sister, attempted to assert his claim to the throne with a band of gladiators. After his initial savagery, he met with a fitting end, for on the twenty-eighth day, he was crushed by the generals of Magnentius and was punished. His head was carried around the city on a spear, and there were severe proscriptions and massacres of the nobility.

12. Not much afterwards, Magnentius was defeated in battle near Mursa and was almost captured. In this battle, vast resources of the Roman Empire, which would have been suitable for any external war and could have provided many triumphs and much security, were consumed. Soon, Gallus, the son of Constantius' uncle, was appointed by Constantius as Caesar to the East. Magnentius, having been defeated in several battles, took his own life near Lugdunum, in the third year and seventh month of his reign, as did his brother, whom he had sent as Caesar to watch over Gaul, in Senones.

13. Also during this time, Gallus Caesar was slain by Constantius after many cruel deeds. He was savage by nature and would have been quite prone to tyranny had he been allowed to rule in his own right. Silanus, who was revolting in Gaul, was killed as well within thirty days. At this time, Constantius was the sole leader and Augustus of the Roman Empire.

14. Soon, after giving his sister in marriage to his cousin Julian (the brother of Gallus), he sent Julian as Caesar to Gaul. This was a time when the barbarians had stormed many towns and besieged others. There was horrible destruction everywhere, and the Roman Empire was tottering on the brink of disaster. With modest forces, Julian killed vast numbers of the Alamanni near Argentoratum, a city of Gaul. He captured their most distinguished king and recovered Gaul. Afterwards, Julian again had great accomplishments against the barbarians. The Germans were pushed beyond the Rhine, and the Roman Empire was restored to its former boundaries.

15. Not much later, when the German armies were being withdrawn from the defense of Gaul, Julian was made emperor by the will of the soldiers. After the span of a year, Julian set out to occupy Illyricum while Constantius was engaged in war with the Parthians. After learning of this, Constantius, while returning to the civil war, died on the march between Cilicia and Cappadocia, in the thirty-eighth year of his reign and forty-fifth year of his life. He gained enrollment among the gods. He was a gentle man of admirable mental calmness who was too trusting in his friends and relatives, and later, too obedient to his wives. In the early years of his reign, he conducted himself with great modesty. He enriched his friends and allowed none to go unhonored whose services he found industrious. He was somewhat inclined to severity if the suspicion of revolt was aroused in him, but mild the rest of the time. His fortune in war was more worthy of praise in civil wars than in foreign ones.

16. Henceforth, Julian gained control of affairs, and after vast preparation, launched a war against the Parthians. I too was present in this expedition. He accepted the surrender of, or took by force, several towns and strongholds of the Persians. He laid waste Assyria and had a fixed camp for a long time near Ctesiphon. As he was returning victorious, he entered several battles rashly and was killed by the hand of an enemy, on June 26th, in the seventh year of his reign, in the thirty-second year of his life, and was enrolled among the gods. He was an admirable man who would have governed the state with distinction had the fates allowed it. He was especially well-educated in liberal disciplines and so learned in Greek, that his knowledge of Latin did not compare. He possessed great and ready eloquence, a tenacious memory, and in certain respects, was more similar to a philosopher. He was kind to his friends, but less diligent than such a chief ought to have been; for there were some who damaged his reputation. He was most just towards the people of the provinces and exercised restraint on taxes as much as possible. He was civil to all and had only moderate concern for the treasury. He was eager for glory but too spirited in its pursuit. He was quite repressive of the Christian religion, but abstained from shedding blood, and was not unlike Marcus Aurelius, whom he was eager to emulate.

17. After him, Jovian, who was then serving as a bodyguard, was selected to rule by the will of the army. He was known to the soldiers more for the excellent reputation of his father than for anything he had done. Since things were in turmoil at this time with the army struggling from a lack of provisions and Jovian having been defeated in two battles by the Persians, he made peace, an ignoble but indeed necessary peace, with Shapur. He was penalized in territory, giving up part of the Roman Empire. This occurrence, in the nearly one thousand, one hundred and eighteen years since the founding of the Roman Empire, had never happened before him. Although our legions were sent under the yoke at Caudium by Pontius Telesinus, near Numantia in Spain, and in Numidia, no territory was surrendered. This condition of peace would not have been totally reprehensible if he had wished, when he renewed his strength, to break the treaty, as was done by the Romans in all those wars which I have mentioned; for wars were waged immediately against the Samnites, Numantians, and Numidians, and the peace was not ratified. But Jovian, as long as he feared a rival in power, thought too little of glory while he remained in the East. After undertaking a march and heading towards Illyricum, he died suddenly on the borders of Galatia. He was a man who in other times was neither unenergetic nor unwise.

18. Many are of the opinion that he passed away from acute indigestion, for he had indulged in sumptuous dishes while dining. Others believed it was from the odor of his bedroom, which was dangerous to one resting in it because of a recent coating of limestone. Still others attributed it to too many charcoals, many of which he had ordered to be piled high due to the severe cold. He died in the seventh month of his reign, on February 17th, in the thirty-third year of his life. Thanks to the kindness of the emperors who succeeded him, he was enrolled among the gods; for he was quite inclined to civility and very liberal by nature.

This was the state of the Roman Empire when this same Jovian, along with Varronianus, were consuls, in the one thousand, one hundred and eighteenth year since the founding of the city. Since we have arrived at renowned chiefs worthy of veneration, I will put an end to this work, as the remaining things must be told in a loftier style. I am not so much setting them aside now as reserving them for a higher effort of writing.

Epilogue

Eutropius' history concludes around the year 370. Emperor Valens, to whom this history was dedicated, met his end in the Roman disaster at Adrianople in 378. The empire in the West would hang on for almost another century. Finally, in the year 476, Odoacer the barbarian deposed the emperor Romulus Augustus, thus bringing the empire in the West to an end.

The empire in the East, the Byzantine Empire, would last for almost another thousand years. It came to an end in 1453 with the seige and capture of Constantinople, today's Istanbul, by the Ottoman sultan Mehmed II.